우주로 간 스탠리

우주로 간 스탠리
(Stanley in Space)

1판 1쇄   2017년 9월 4일
2판 1쇄   2025년 1월 6일

지은이   Jeff Brown
기획   이수영
책임편집   김보경 정소이
콘텐츠제작및감수   롱테일 교육 연구소
저작권   명채린
마케팅   두잉글 사업본부

펴낸이   이수영
펴낸곳   롱테일북스
출판등록   제2015-000191호
주소   04033 서울특별시 마포구 양화로 113, 3층(서교동, 순흥빌딩)
전자메일   help@ltinc.net

이 도서는 대한민국에서 제작되었습니다.
롱테일북스는 롱테일㈜의 출판 브랜드입니다.

ISBN 979-11-93992-41-8 14740

CONTENTS

미국 초등학생 사이에서 저스틴 비버보다 더 유명한 소년, 플랫 스탠리!

『플랫 스탠리(Flat Stanley)』 시리즈는 미국의 작가 제프 브라운(Jeff Brown)이 쓴 책으로, 한밤중에 몸 위로 떨어진 거대한 게시판에 눌려 납작해진(flat) 스탠리가 겪는 다양한 모험을 담고 있습니다. 플랫 스탠리는 아동 도서이지만 부모님들과 선생님들에게도 큰 사랑을 받으며, 출간된 지 50년이 넘은 지금까지 여러 세대를 아우르며 독자들에게 재미를 주고 있습니다. 미국에서만 100만 부 이상 판매된 『플랫 스탠리』 시리즈는 기존 챕터북 시리즈와 함께 플랫 스탠리의 세계 모험(Flat Stanley's Worldwide Adventures) 시리즈, 리더스북 등 다양한 형태로 출판되었고, 여러 언어로 번역되어 전 세계 독자들의 마음을 사로잡았습니다. 주인공 스탠리가 그려진 종이 인형을 만들어 이를 우편으로 원하는 사람에게 보내는 플랫 스탠리 프로젝트(The Flat Stanley Project)가 1995년에 시작된 이후, 이 책은 더 많은 관심을 받게 되었습니다. 유명 연예인은 물론 오바마 대통령까지 이 종이 인형과 함께 사진을 찍어 공유하는 등, 수많은 사례를 통해 시리즈의 높은 인기를 짐작할 수 있습니다.

이러한 『플랫 스탠리』 시리즈는 한국에서도 널리 알려져 '엄마표·아빠표 영어'를 진행하는 부모님과 초보 영어 학습자라면 반드시 읽어야 하는 영어원서로 자리 잡았습니다. 렉사일 지수가 최대 640L인 플랫 스탠리는 간결하지만 필수적인 어휘로 쓰여, 영어원서가 친숙하지 않은 학습자들에게도 즐거운 원서 읽기 경험을 선사할 것입니다.

번역과 단어장이 포함된 워크북, 그리고 오디오북까지 담긴 풀 패키지!

이 책은 영어원서 『플랫 스탠리』 시리즈에, 탁월한 학습 효과를 거둘 수 있도록 다양한 콘텐츠를 덧붙인 책입니다.

- 영어원서: 본문에 나온 어려운 어휘에 볼드 처리가 되어 있어 단어를 더욱 분명하게 인지할 수 있고, 문맥에 따른 자연스러운 암기 효과를 얻을 수 있습니다.
- 단어장: 원서에 볼드 처리된 어휘의 의미가 완벽하게 정리되어 있어 사전 없이 원서를 수월하게 읽을 수 있으며, 반복해서 등장하는 단어에 '복습' 표기를 하여 자연스럽게 복습을 돕도록 구성했습니다.

- 번역: 영문과 비교할 수 있도록 직역에 가까운 번역을 담았습니다. 원서 읽기에 익숙하지 않은 초보 학습자도 어려움 없이 내용을 파악할 수 있습니다.
- 퀴즈: 챕터별로 내용을 확인하는 이해력 점검 퀴즈가 들어 있습니다.
- 오디오북: 미국 현지에서 판매 중인 빠른 속도의 오디오북(분당 약 145단어)과 국내에서 녹음된 따라 읽기용 오디오북(분당 약 110단어)을 기본으로 포함하고 있어, 듣기 훈련은 물론 소리 내어 읽기에까지 폭넓게 활용할 수 있습니다.

이 책의 수준과 타깃 독자
- 미국 원어민 기준: 유치원 ~ 초등학교 저학년
- 한국 학습자 기준: 초등학교 저학년 ~ 중학생
- 영어원서 완독 경험이 없는 초보 영어 학습자
- 도서 분량: 약 5,900단어
- 비슷한 수준의 다른 챕터북: Arthur Chapter Book,★ The Zack Files,★ Tales from the Odyssey,★ Junie B. Jones,★ Magic Tree House, Marvin Redpost

  ★ 「롱테일 에디션」으로 출간된 도서

『플랫 스탠리』 이렇게 읽어 보세요!

- **단어 암기는 이렇게!** 처음 리딩을 시작하기 전, 오늘 읽을 챕터에 나오는 단어들을 눈으로 쭉 훑어봅니다. 모르는 단어는 좀 더 주의 깊게 보되, 손으로 쓰면서 완벽하게 암기할 필요는 없습니다. 본문을 읽으면서 이 단어를 다시 만나게 되는데, 그 과정에서 단어의 쓰임새와 어감을 자연스럽게 익히게 됩니다. 이렇게 책을 읽은 후에 단어를 다시 한번 복습하세요. 복습할 때는 중요하다고 생각하는 단어들을 손으로 쓰면서 꼼꼼하게 외우는 것도 좋습니다. 이런 방식으로 책을 읽으면 많은 단어를 빠르고 부담 없이 익힐 수 있습니다.

- **리딩할 때는 리딩에만 집중하자!** 원서를 읽는 중간중간 모르는 단어가 나온다고 워크북을 바로 펼쳐 보거나, 곧바로 번역을 찾아보는 것은 크게 도움이 되지 않습니다. 모르는 단어나 이해되지 않는 문장들은 따로 가볍게 표시만 해 두고, 전체적인 맥락을 파악하며 속도감 있게 읽어 나가세요. 리딩을 할 때는 속

도에 대한 긴장감을 잃지 않으면서 리딩에만 집중하는 것이 좋습니다. 모르는 단어와 문장은 리딩을 마친 후에 한꺼번에 정리하는 '리뷰' 시간을 통해 점검하는 시간을 가지면 됩니다. 리뷰를 할 때는 번역은 물론 단어장과 사전도 꼼꼼하게 확인하면서 어떤 이유에서 이해가 되지 않았는지 생각해 봅니다.

- **번역 활용은 이렇게!** 이해가 가지 않는 문장은 번역을 통해서 그 의미를 파악할 수 있습니다. 하지만 한국어와 영어는 정확히 1:1 대응이 되지 않기 때문에 번역을 활용하는 데에도 지혜가 필요합니다. 의역이 된 부분까지 억지로 의미를 대응해서 이해하려고 하기보다, 어떻게 그런 의미가 만들어진 것인지 추측하면서 번역은 참고 자료로 활용하는 것이 좋습니다.

- **듣기 훈련은 이렇게!** 리스닝 실력을 향상시키고 싶다면 오디오북을 적극적으로 활용해 보세요. 처음에는 오디오북을 틀어 놓고 눈으로 해당 내용을 따라 읽으면서 훈련을 하고, 이것이 익숙해지면 오디오북만 틀어 놓고 '귀를 통해' 책을 읽어 보세요. 눈으로 읽지 않은 책이라도 귀를 통해 이해할 수 있을 정도가 되면, 이후에 영어 듣기로 어려움을 겪는 일은 거의 없을 것입니다.

- **소리 내어 읽고 녹음하자!** 이 책은 특히 소리 내어 읽기(voice reading)에 최적화된 문장 길이와 구조를 가지고 있습니다. 오디오북 기본 구성에 포함된 '따라 읽기용' 오디오북을 활용해 소리 내어 읽기 훈련을 시작해 보세요! 내가 읽은 것을 녹음하고 들어보는 과정을 통해 자연스럽게 어휘와 표현을 복습하고, 의식적·무의식적으로 발음을 교정하게 됩니다. 이렇게 영어로 소리를 만들어 본 경험은 이후 탄탄한 스피킹 실력의 밑거름이 될 것입니다.

- **2~3번 반복해서 읽자!** 영어 초보자라면 처음부터 완벽하게 이해하려고 하는 것보다는 2~3회 반복해서 읽을 것을 추천합니다. 처음 원서를 읽을 때는 생소한 단어들과 스토리 때문에 내용 파악에 급급할 수밖에 없습니다. 하지만 일단 내용을 파악한 후에 다시 읽으면 문장 구조나 어휘의 활용에 더 집중하게 되고, 원서를 더 깊이 있게 읽을 수 있습니다. 그 과정에서 리딩 속도에 탄력이 붙고 리딩 실력 또한 더 확고히 다지게 됩니다.

- **'시리즈'로 꾸준히 읽자!** 한 작가의 책을 시리즈로 읽는 것 또한 영어 실력 향상에 큰 도움이 됩니다. 같은 등장인물이 다시 나오기 때문에 내용 파악이 더 수월할 뿐 아니라, 작가가 사용하는 어휘와 표현들도 반복되기 때문에 탁월한 복습 효과까지 얻을 수 있습니다. 롱테일북스의 『플랫 스탠리』시리즈는 현재 6권, 총 35,700단어 분량이 출간되어 있습니다. 시리즈를 꾸준히 읽다 보면 영어 실력이 자연스럽게 향상될 것입니다.

원서 본문 구성

<u>내용이 담긴 원서 본문입니다.</u>
원어민이 읽는 일반 원서와 같은 텍스트지만, 암기해야 할 중요 어휘들은 볼드체로 표시되어 있습니다. 이 어휘들은 지금 들고 계신 워크북에 챕터별로 정리되어 있습니다.

학습 심리학 연구 결과에 따르면, 한 단어씩 따로 외우는 단어 암기는 거의 효과가 없다고 합니다. 단어를 제대로 외우기 위해서는 문맥(context) 속에서 단어를 암기해야 하며, 한 단어당 문맥 속에서 15번 이상 마주칠 때 완벽하게 암기할 수 있다고 합니다.
이 책의 본문에서는 중요 어휘를 볼드체로 강조하여, 문맥 속의 단어들을 더 확실히 인지(word cognition in context)하도록 돕고 있습니다. 또한 대부분의 중요 단어들은 다른 챕터에서도 반복해서 등장하기 때문에 이 책을 읽는 것만으로도 자연스럽게 어휘력을 향상시킬 수 있습니다.

본문 하단에는 내용 이해를 돕기 위한 '각주'가 첨가되어 있습니다. 각주는 굳이 암기할 필요는 없지만, 알아 두면 도움이 될 만한 정보를 설명하고 있습니다. 각주를 참고하면 스토리를 더 깊이 있게 이해할 수 있어 원서를 읽는 재미가 배가됩니다.

워크북(Workbook) 구성

Check Your Reading Speed
해당 챕터의 단어 수가 기록되어 있어, 리딩 속도를 측정할 수 있습니다. 특히 리딩 속도를 중시하는 독자들이 유용하게 사용할 수 있습니다.

Build Your Vocabulary
본문에 볼드 표시되어 있는 단어들이 정리되어 있습니다. 리딩 전·후에 반복해서 보면 원서를 더욱 쉽게 읽을 수 있고, 어휘력도 빠르게 향상될 것입니다.

단어는 〈스펠링 – 빈도 – 발음기호 – 품사 – 한글 뜻 – 영문 뜻〉 순서로 표기되어 있으며 빈도 표시(★)가 많을수록 필수 어휘입니다. 반복해서 등장하는 단어는 빈도 대신 '복습'으로 표기되어 있습니다. 품사는 아래와 같이 표기했습니다.

n. 명사 ｜ a. 형용사 ｜ ad. 부사 ｜ v. 동사
conj. 접속사 ｜ prep. 전치사 ｜ int. 감탄사 ｜ idiom 숙어 및 관용구

Comprehension Quiz
간단한 퀴즈를 통해 읽은 내용에 대한 이해력을 점검해 볼 수 있습니다.

한국어 번역
영문과 비교할 수 있도록 최대한 직역에 가까운 번역을 담았습니다.

오디오북 구성

이 책에는 '듣기 훈련'과 '소리 내어 읽기 훈련'을 위한 2가지 종류의 오디오북이
기본으로 포함되어 있습니다.

- 듣기 훈련용 오디오북: 분당 145단어 속도 (미국 현지에서 판매 중인 오디오북)
- 따라 읽기용 오디오북: 분당 110단어 속도 (소리 내어 읽기 훈련용 오디오북)

 QR코드를 인식하여 따라 읽기용 & 듣기 훈련용 두 가지 오디오북을 들어
보세요! 더불어 롱테일북스 홈페이지 (www.longtailbooks.co.kr)에서도
오디오북 MP3 파일을 다운로드 받을 수 있습니다.

The Call

1. Why do Mr. and Mrs. Lambchop like ordinary days?

A. They can do chores at home on ordinary days.

B. They can rest at home on ordinary days.

C. Ordinary days are not troublesome.

D. Ordinary days can be very exciting.

2. Why did Stanley tell the President that he was the King of France?

A. He wanted the President to think he was an important person.

B. He didn't believe the President of the United States was really calling.

C. He thought the President would appreciate his joke.

D. He figured the President wouldn't know he was lying.

3. Why did the President go on TV?

A. To get Stanley's attention

B. To talk about some serious national news

C. To introduce the Tom Toad Show

D. To give a long speech

4. How did the Lambchop family react after seeing the President on TV?

A. Stanley was proud of being mentioned by the President.

B. Mr. Lambchop was confused about what the President's message meant.

C. Arthur was worried that Stanley might get arrested.

D. Mrs. Lambchop was upset that Stanley hadn't mentioned his phone call with the President before.

5. What is the President going to do?

A. He is going to visit the Lambchop family.

B. He is going to send the Lambchop family on a trip to France.

C. He is going to give the Lambchop family a tour around Washington, D.C.

D. He is going to send a plane to pick up the Lambchop family.

Check Your Reading Speed
1분에 몇 단어를 읽는지 리딩 속도를 측정해보세요.

$$\frac{584 \text{ words}}{\text{reading time ( ) sec}} \times 60 = (\quad) \text{ WPM}$$

Build Your Vocabulary

farness [fá:rnis] n. 멀리 떨어짐; 아득함
Farness is the condition of being far off.

* **planet** [plǽnit] n. [천문] 행성
A planet is a large, round object in space that moves around a star.

* **mention** [ménʃən] v. 말하다, 언급하다; n. 언급, 거론
If you mention something, you say something about it, usually briefly.

wallpaper [wɔ́:lpeipər] n. 벽지; v. 벽지를 바르다
Wallpaper is thick colored or patterned paper that is used for covering and decorating the walls of rooms.

* **stir** [stə:r] v. 젓다, (저어 가며) 섞다; 약간 움직이다; n. 동요, 충격; 젓기
If you stir a liquid or other substance, you move it around or mix it in a container using something such as a spoon.

* **paste** [peist] n. (밀가루 등으로 만든) 풀, 반죽; v. 풀로 붙이다
Paste is a soft, wet, sticky mixture of a substance and a liquid, which can be spread easily. Some types of paste are used to stick things together.

* **troublesome** [trʌ́blsəm] a. 골칫거리인, 고질적인
You use troublesome to describe something or someone that causes annoying problems or difficulties.

bulletin board [búlətin bɔːrd] n. 게시판
A bulletin board is a board which is usually attached to a wall in order to display notices giving information about something.

settle [setl] v. (떨어져·내려) 앉다; 자리를 잡다; 해결하다
If something settles or if you settle it, it sinks slowly down and becomes still.

overnight [òuvərnáit] ad. 밤사이에, 하룻밤 동안
If something happens overnight, it happens throughout the night or at some point during the night.

grant [grænt] v. 승인하다, 허락하다; 인정하다; n. 보조금
If someone in authority grants you something, or if something is granted to you, you are allowed to have it.

spring [spriŋ] v. (sprung/sprang–sprung) (~의) 출신이다; 휙 움직이다; (갑자기) 뛰어오르다; n. 봄; 생기, 활기; 샘
If one thing springs from another thing, it is the result of it.

dear [diər] n. 여보, 당신; 얘야; int. 이런!, 맙소사!; a. 사랑하는; ~에게
You can call someone dear as a sign of affection.

smooth [smuːð] v. 매끈하게 하다; a. 매끈한; 순조로운
If you smooth something, you move your hands over its surface to make it smooth and flat.

ordinary [ɔ́ːrdənèri] a. 보통의, 평범한
Ordinary people or things are normal and not special or different in any way.

sporty [spɔ́ːrti] a. 스포츠를 잘하는
Someone who is sporty likes playing sports.

splash [splæʃ] n. 첨벙 하는 소리; (어디에 떨어지는) 방울; v. (물 등을) 끼얹다; (액체가) 후두둑 떨어지다
A splash is the sound made when something hits water or falls into it.

residence [rézədəns] n. 주택, 거주지; 거주, 상주
Your place of residence is the place where you live.

president [prézədənt] n. 대통령; 회장
The president of a country that has no king or queen is the person who is the head of state of that country.

joke [dʒouk] n. 농담; 웃음거리; v. 농담하다; 농담 삼아 말하다
A joke is something that is said or done to make you laugh, for example a funny story.

keep one's eye on idiom ~에서 눈을 떼지 않다; 경계하다
If you keep your eyes on someone or something, you are watching them carefully and closely.

fellow [félou] n. 녀석, 친구; 동료; a. 동료의
A fellow is a man or boy.

hang up idiom 전화를 끊다
If you hang up the phone or hang up on someone, you end a telephone conversation, often very suddenly.

rest [rest] n. 나머지; 휴식; v. 쉬다; 놓이다, (~에) 있다
The rest is used to refer to all the parts of something or all the things in a group that remain or that you have not already mentioned.

hay [hei] n. 건초
Hay is grass which has been cut and dried so that it can be used to feed animals.

mindful [máindfəl] a. ~을 염두에 두는, ~에 유념하는
If you are mindful of something, you think about it and consider it when taking action.

vanish [vǽniʃ] v. 사라지다, 없어지다; 모습을 감추다
If someone or something vanishes, they disappear suddenly or in a way that cannot be explained.

‡ **screen** [skri:n] n. (텔레비전·컴퓨터) 화면; 칸막이; v. 가리다, 차단하다
A screen is a flat vertical surface on which pictures or words are shown.

‡ **flag** [flæg] n. 기, 깃발; v. 표시를 하다; 지치다; 약해지다
A flag is a piece of cloth which can be attached to a pole and which is used as a sign, signal, or symbol of something, especially of a particular country.

‡ **announcer** [ənáunsər] n. (프로그램) 방송 진행자
An announcer is someone who introduces programs on radio or television or who reads the text of a radio or television advertisement.

‡ **interrupt** [intərʌ́pt] v. 중단시키다; (말·행동을) 방해하다; 차단하다
If someone or something interrupts a process or activity, they stop it for a period of time.

‡ **realize** [rí:əlàiz] v. 깨닫다, 알아차리다; 실현하다
If you realize that something is true, you become aware of that fact or understand it.

‡ **particular** [pərtíkjulər] a. 특정한; 특별한; 까다로운; n. 자세한 사실
You use particular to emphasize that you are talking about one thing or one kind of thing rather than other similar ones.

‡ **exclaim** [ikskléim] v. 소리치다, 외치다
If you exclaim, you cry out suddenly in surprise, strong emotion, or pain.

gosh [gaʃ] int. (놀람·기쁨을 나타내어) 어머!, 뭐라고!
Some people say 'Gosh' when they are surprised.

‡ **jail** [dʒeil] n. 교도소, 감옥; v. 수감하다
A jail is a place where criminals are kept in order to punish them, or where people waiting to be tried are kept.

smarty [smá:rti] n. 잘난 체하는 놈
If you describe someone as a smarty, you dislike the fact that they think they are very clever and always have an answer for everything.

get hold of idiom ~와 연락하다; ~을 찾다
If you get hold of someone, you manage to contact them.

hold on idiom 기다려, 멈춰; ~을 계속 잡고 있다
If you say 'hold on' to someone, you ask them to wait or stop for a short time.

＊**private** [práivət] a. 개인 소유의; 사적인; 사생활의
Your private things belong only to you, or may only be used by you.

＊**fetch** [feʧ] v. 가지고 오다, 데리고 오다; (특정 가격에) 팔리다; n. 가져옴, 데려옴
If you fetch something or someone, you go and get them from the place where they are.

＊**gasp** [gæsp] v. 숨이 턱 막히다, 헉 하고 숨을 쉬다; n. 헉 하는 소리를 냄
When you gasp, you take a short quick breath through your mouth, especially when you are surprised, shocked, or in pain.

＊**chuckle** [ʧʌkl] v. 킬킬 웃다; 빙그레 웃다; n. 킬킬거림; 속으로 웃기
When you chuckle, you laugh quietly.

＊**include** [inklú:d] v. 포함하다; ~을 (~에) 포함시키다
If one thing includes another thing, it has the other thing as one of its parts.

Washington

1. What do the Tyrrans want?

   A. They want to build a spaceship.

   B. They want to travel to outer space.

   C. They want to move to Earth.

   D. They want to meet people from Earth.

2. What is the *Star Scout?*

   A. The name of a planet

   B. The name of a mission

   C. The name of a spaceship

   D. Stanley's new nickname

3. Why does the President want to send Stanley to Tyrra?

A. Stanley has been on adventures before.

B. Stanley knows how to use scientific equipment.

C. Stanley is the most famous boy in America.

D. Stanley is the most normal boy in America.

4. Who has traveled in the top-secret spaceship before?

A. Dr. Herman Schwartz

B. Polly the parrot

C. The President of the United States

D. The Secret Service

5. What will the Lambchops do?

A. They will make a decision about the mission later.

B. They will go on a family vacation to the seaside.

C. They will have tea with the Queen of England.

D. They will go to Tyrra all together.

Check Your Reading Speed

1분에 몇 단어를 읽는지 리딩 속도를 측정해보세요.

$$\frac{717 \text{ words}}{\text{reading time ( ) sec}} \times 60 = (\qquad) \text{ WPM}$$

Build Your Vocabulary

★ **oval** [óuvəl] a. 타원형의; n. 타원형
Oval things have a shape that is like a circle but is wider in one direction than the other.

복습 **president** [prézədənt] n. 대통령; 회장
The president of a country that has no king or queen is the person who is the head of state of that country.

복습 **chuckle** [tʃʌkl] v. 킬킬 웃다; 빙그레 웃다; n. 킬킬거림; 속으로 웃기
When you chuckle, you laugh quietly.

★ **bet** [bet] v. ~이 틀림없다; (내기 등에) 돈을 걸다; n. 내기; 짐작, 추측
You use expressions such as 'I bet,' 'I'll bet,' and 'you can bet' to indicate that you are sure something is true.

복습 **planet** [plǽnit] n. [천문] 행성
A planet is a large, round object in space that moves around a star.

outer space [autər spéis] n. (대기권 외) 우주 공간
Outer space is the area outside the Earth's atmosphere where the other planets and stars are situated.

★★ **imagine** [imǽdʒin] v. 상상하다, (마음속으로) 그리다
If you imagine something, you think about it and your mind forms a picture or idea of it.

^복^습 **exclaim** [ikskléim] v. 소리치다, 외치다
If you exclaim, you cry out suddenly in surprise, strong emotion, or pain.

⋆ **friendly** [fréndli] a. (행동이) 친절한, 우호적인; 상냥한, 다정한
If someone is friendly, they behave in a pleasant, kind way, and like to be with other people.

⋆ **tone** [toun] n. 어조; 음조, 음색
Someone's tone is a quality in their voice which shows what they are feeling or thinking.

⋆ **peaceful** [píːsfəl] a. 평화적인; 평화로운
Peaceful people are not violent and try to avoid quarrelling or fighting with other people.

⋆ **reveal** [rivíːl] v. (보이지 않던 것을) 드러내 보이다; (비밀 등을) 밝히다
If you reveal something that has been out of sight, you uncover it so that people can see it.

⋆⋆ **dress** [dres] v. 옷을 입다; n. 드레스; 옷
When you dress or dress yourself, you put on clothes.

⋆ **crown** [kraun] n. 왕관; 왕위, 왕권; v. 왕관을 씌우다, 왕위에 앉히다
A crown is a circular ornament, usually made of gold and jewels, which a king or queen wears on their head at official ceremonies.

⋆ **recognize** [rékəgnàiz] v. 알아보다; 인식하다; 공인하다
If you recognize someone or something, you know who that person is or what that thing is.

at once idiom 즉시; 동시에
If you do something at once, you do it immediately.

⋆ **banquet** [bǽŋkwit] n. 연회
A banquet is a grand formal dinner.

⋆ **beg** [beg] v. 간청하다, 애원하다; 구걸하다
If you beg someone to do something, you ask them very anxiously or eagerly to do it.

pardon [paːrdn] int. 뭐라고요; n. 용서; v. 용서하다 (beg pardon idiom 뭐라고요)
You say 'I beg your pardon' as a way of apologizing for accidentally doing
something wrong, such as disturbing someone or making a mistake.

madhouse [mǽdhaus] n. 정신없는 곳
If you describe a place or situation as a madhouse, you mean that it is
full of confusion and noise.

fancy [fǽnsi] a. 고급의; 장식이 많은, 색깔이 화려한; v. 생각하다, 상상하다
If you describe something as fancy, you mean that it is very expensive
or of very high quality, and you often dislike it because of this.

scout [skaut] n. 정찰병; 스카우트; v. (무엇을 찾아) 돌아다니다; 정찰하다
A scout is someone who is sent to an area of countryside to find out the
position of an enemy army.

lean [liːn] v. 기울이다, (몸을) 숙이다; ~에 기대다; a. 군살이 없는, 호리호리한
When you lean in a particular direction, you bend your body in that
direction.

spaceship [spéisʃip] n. 우주선
A spaceship is a rocket or other vehicle that carries people through space.

ordinary [ɔ́ːrdənèri] a. 보통의, 평범한
Ordinary people or things are normal and not special or different in any
way.

gasp [gæsp] v. 숨이 턱 막히다, 헉 하고 숨을 쉬다; n. 헉 하는 소리를 냄
When you gasp, you take a short quick breath through your mouth,
especially when you are surprised, shocked, or in pain.

alien [éiljən] n. 외계인, 우주인; a. 외계의; 생경한; 이질적인
In science fiction, an alien is a creature from outer space.

race [reis] n. 인종, 종족; 경주; 경쟁; v. 쏜살같이 가다; 경주하다
A race is one of the major groups which human beings can be divided
into according to their physical features, such as the color of their skin.

draw in a breath idiom (심)호흡하다
If you draw in a breath, you breathe deeply or quickly.

adventure [ædvénʧər] n. 모험; 모험심
If someone has an adventure, they become involved in an unusual, exciting, and rather dangerous journey or series of events.

rob [rab] v. 도둑질하다 (robber n. 강도)
A robber is someone who steals money or property from a bank, a shop, or a vehicle, often by using force or threats.

interrupt [intərʌ́pt] v. (말·행동을) 방해하다; 중단시키다; 차단하다
If you interrupt someone who is speaking, you say or do something that causes them to stop.

concern [kənsə́:rn] n. 우려, 걱정; 관심사; v. 걱정스럽게 하다; 관련되다
Concern is worry about a situation.

mission [míʃən] n. 우주 비행; 임무
A mission is a special journey made by a military airplane or space rocket.

goodness [gúdnis] int. 와!, 어머나!, 맙소사!; n. 신; 선량함
People sometimes say 'goodness' or 'my goodness' to express surprise.

take care idiom ~을 처리하다; ~을 돌보다
If you take care to do something, you make sure that you do it.

latest [léitist] a. 최근의
You use latest to describe something that is the most recent thing of its kind.

scientific [sàiəntífik] a. 과학의; 과학적인, 체계적인
Scientific is used to describe things that relate to science or to a particular science.

equipment [ikwípmənt] n. 장비, 용품; 설비
Equipment consists of the things which are used for a particular purpose, for example a hobby or job.

automatic [ɔ̀:təmǽtik] a. 자동의; 무의식적인, 반사적인
An automatic machine or device is one which has controls that enable it to perform a task without needing to be constantly operated by a person.

pilot [páilət] n. 조종사, 비행사
A pilot is a person who is trained to fly an aircraft.

passenger [pǽsəndʒər] n. 승객
A passenger in a vehicle such as a bus, boat, or plane is a person who is travelling in it, but who is not driving it or working on it.

satisfy [sǽtisfài] v. 만족시키다; 충족시키다 (satisfied a. 만족하는, 흡족해하는)
If you are satisfied with something, you are happy because you have got what you wanted or needed.

clever [klévər] a. 영리한, 똑똑한; 기발한, 재치 있는
Someone who is clever is intelligent and able to understand things easily or plan things well.

aboard [əbɔ́:rd] ad. (배·기차·비행기 등에) 탄, 탑승한
If you are aboard a ship or plane, you are on it or in it.

beard [biərd] n. 턱수염 (bearded a. 수염이 있는)
A man's beard is the hair that grows on his chin and cheeks.

cage [keidʒ] n. 우리, 새장; v. 우리에 가두다 (birdcage n. 새장)
A cage is a structure of wire or metal bars in which birds or animals are kept.

cloth [klɔ:θ] n. 천
A cloth is a piece of cloth which you use for a particular purpose, such as cleaning something or covering something.

bow [bau] v. (허리를 굽혀) 절하다; n. 절, (고개 숙여 하는) 인사
When you bow to someone, you briefly bend your body toward them as a formal way of greeting them or showing respect.

parrot [pǽrət] n. [동물] 앵무새
A parrot is a tropical bird with a curved beak and brightly-colored or gray feathers.

folk [fouk] n. (pl.) (일반적인) 사람들; (pl.) 여러분, 얘들아; (pl.) 부모
You can refer to people as folk or folks.

a piece of cake idiom 식은 죽 먹기
If you think something is very easy to do, you can say that it is a piece of cake.

terrific [tərífik] a. 아주 좋은, 멋진, 훌륭한; (양·정도 등이) 엄청난
If you describe something or someone as terrific, you are very pleased with them or very impressed by them.

reassure [riːəʃúər] v. 안심시키다 (reassuring a. 안심시키는, 걱정을 없애 주는)
If you find someone's words or actions reassuring, they make you feel less worried about something.

out of the question idiom 불가능한, 의논해 봐야 소용없는
If you say that something is out of the question, you are emphasizing that it is completely impossible or unacceptable.

crowd [kraud] v. 가득 메우다; (생각이 마음속에) 밀려오다; n. 사람들, 군중
If a group of people crowd a place, there are so many of them there that it is full.

skimp [skimp] v. (돈·시간 등을) 지나치게 아끼다
If you skimp on something, you use less time, money, or material for it than you really need, so that the result is not good enough.

baggage [bǽgidʒ] n. 수하물
Your baggage consists of the bags that you take with you when you travel.

have in mind idiom ~을 염두에 두다, 생각하다
If you have it in mind to do something, you intend or want to do it.

seaside [síːsaid] n. (휴가 등을 위해 찾는) 해변
You can refer to an area that is close to the sea, especially one where people go for their holidays, as the seaside.

sake [seik] n. (~을) 위함 (for heaven's sake idiom 제발, 부디, 맙소사)
Some people use expressions such as 'for heaven's sake' or 'for God's sake' in order to express annoyance or impatience, or to add force to a question or request.

anon [ənán] ad. 곧
Anon means quite soon.

peeved [piːvd] a. 짜증이 난
If you are peeved about something, you are annoyed about it.

Taking Off

1. **What was Stanley's job during takeoff?**

   A. To count down from ten to zero

   B. To press the "Start" button after the countdown

   C. To tell Mission Control when everyone was ready to go

   D. To check that everyone's seatbelts were fastened

2. **What was Stanley thinking during the countdown?**

   A. He was wondering if the Tyrrans were just ordinary aliens.

   B. He was wondering if the Tyrrans would be disappointed to meet the Lambchops.

   C. He was wondering if the Tyrrans had heard of him before.

   D. He was wondering if it would be difficult to find the Tyrrans.

3. How was Mr. Lambchop feeling?

A. He was very excited.

B. He was really jealous.

C. He was a little overwhelmed.

D. He was a bit bored.

4. What was one thing that Mrs. Lambchop was thinking about?

A. She was thinking about how fun the training had been.

B. She was thinking about how awful the training had been.

C. She was thinking about how drab the spaceship still looked.

D. She was thinking about how pretty the spaceship now looked.

5. How was Arthur feeling?

A. He was relieved to have finished all the training.

B. He was sad to be leaving Earth.

C. He was happy to be going on a new adventure.

D. He was worried about whether he was ready for the mission.

Check Your Reading Speed

1분에 몇 단어를 읽는지 리딩 속도를 측정해보세요.

$$\frac{417 \text{ words}}{\text{reading time ( ) sec}} \times 60 = (\quad) \text{ WPM}$$

Build Your Vocabulary

take off idiom 이륙하다; (서둘러) 떠나다
If a bird or an airplane takes off, it leaves the ground and begins to fly.

mission [míʃən] n. 우주 비행; 임무 (mission control n. 우주 비행 관제 센터)
Mission control is the group of people on Earth who are in charge of a flight by a spacecraft, or the place where these people work.

countdown [káuntdaun] n. 카운트다운; (중요한 행사의) 초읽기
A countdown is the counting aloud of numbers in reverse order before something happens, especially before a spacecraft is launched.

reach [ri:tʃ] v. ~에 이르다; (손·팔을) 뻗다; n. (닿을 수 있는) 거리; 범위
If someone or something has reached a certain stage, level, or amount, they are at that stage, level, or amount.

chief [tʃi:f] a. (계급·직급상) 최고위자인; n. (조직·집단의) 장(長)
Chief is used in the job titles of the most senior worker or workers of a particular kind in an organization.

pilot [páilət] n. 조종사, 비행사
A pilot is a person who is trained to fly an aircraft.

press [pres] v. 누르다; (무엇에) 바짝 대다; 밀다; n. 언론; 인쇄
If you press a button or switch, you push it with your finger in order to make a machine or device work.

§ **scout** [skaut] n. 정찰병; 스카우트; v. (무엇을 찾아) 돌아다니다; 정찰하다
A scout is someone who is sent to an area of countryside to find out the position of an enemy army.

* **blast** [blæst] v. 폭발시키다; (음악이) 쾅쾅 울리다; n. 폭발; (한 줄기의) 강한 바람
(blast off idiom 발사되다)
When a spacecraft blasts off, it leaves the ground and goes up into space.

* **strap** [stræp] v. 끈으로 묶다; 붕대를 감다; n. 끈, 줄, 띠
If you strap something somewhere, you fasten it there with a strap.

hold one's breath idiom (흥분·공포 등으로) 숨을 죽이다
If you say that someone is holding their breath, you mean that they are waiting anxiously or excitedly for something to happen.

stuck-up [stʌk-ʌ́p] a. 거드름 피우는, 거만한
If you say that someone is stuck-up, you mean that are very proud and unfriendly because they think they are very important.

§ **expect** [ikspékt] v. 예상하다, 기대하다
If you are expecting something or someone, you believe that they will be delivered to you or come to you soon.

fix one's eyes on idiom ~을 주시하다, 눈여겨보다
If you fix your eyes or your attention on someone or something, you look straight at them and at nothing else.

* **panel** [pænl] n. (자동차 등의) 계기판; 판; 패널, 자문단
A control panel or instrument panel is a board or surface which contains switches and controls to operate a machine or piece of equipment.

§ **serve** [səːrv] v. (조직·국가 등을 위해) 일하다; (특정한 용도로) 쓰일 수 있다; (상품·서비스를) 제공하다
If you serve your country, an organization, or a person, you do useful work for them.

* **noble** [noubl] a. 고귀한, 숭고한; 귀족의
If you say that something is a noble idea, goal, or action, you admire it because it is based on high moral principles.

‚ unknown [ʌnnóun] a. 알려지지 않은; 유명하지 않은
If something is unknown to you, you have no knowledge of it.

‚ entire [intáiər] a. 전체의, 온
You use entire when you want to emphasize that you are referring to the whole of something.

‚ sigh [sai] v. 한숨을 쉬다, 한숨짓다; 탄식하듯 말하다; n. 한숨
When you sigh, you let out a deep breath, as a way of expressing feelings such as disappointment, tiredness, or pleasure.

fretful [frétfəl] a. 조바심이 나는, 조마조마해하는
If someone is fretful, they behave in a way that shows that they worried or unhappy about something.

spaceship [spéisʃip] n. 우주선
A spaceship is a rocket or other vehicle that carries people through space.

drab [dræb] a. 생기 없는, 칙칙한; 재미없는
If you describe something as drab, you think that it is dull and boring to look at or experience.

‚ physical [fízikəl] a. 육체의; 물질의, 물리적인
Physical qualities, actions, or things are connected with a person's body, rather than with their mind.

‚ jog [dʒag] v. 천천히 달리다, 조깅하다; n. 조깅
If you jog, you run slowly, often as a form of exercise.

‚ require [rikwáiər] v. 필요로 하다, 요구하다
If you require something or if something is required, you need it or it is necessary.

‚ fit [fit] a. 건강한; 적합한, 알맞은; v. (모양·크기가) 맞다; 적절하다
Someone who is fit is healthy and physically strong.

‚ weight [weit] n. 무게, 체중; 무거운 것
The weight of a person or thing is how heavy they are, measured in units such as kilograms, pounds, or tons.

permit [pərmít] v. 허락하다; n. 허가증
If a situation permits something, it makes it possible for that thing to exist, happen, or be done or it provides the opportunity for it.

scale [skeil] n. 저울; 규모, 범위; 눈금; v. 오르다
Scales are a piece of equipment used for weighing things.

alcove [ǽlkouv] n. 작은 방 (shower alcove n. 샤워실)
An alcove is a small area of a room which is formed by one part of a wall being built further back than the rest of the wall.

shade [ʃeid] n. 창문 블라인드; 색조; 그늘; v. 그늘지게 하다, (빛을) 가리다
A shade is a piece of stiff cloth or heavy paper that you can pull down over a window as a covering.

porthole [pɔ́:rthòul] n. (선박·항공기 측면의) 둥근 창
A porthole is a small round window in the side of a ship or aircraft.

blind [blaind] n. (창문에 치는) 블라인드; a. 눈이 먼; 맹목적인; v. 눈이 멀게 만들다
A blind is a roll of cloth or paper which you can pull down over a window as a covering.

magnify [mǽgnəfài] v. 확대하다; 과장하다
To magnify an object means to make it appear larger than it really is, by means of a special lens or mirror.

explore [iksplɔ́:r] v. 탐험하다, 탐사하다; 분석하다 (exploration n. 탐사, 답사)
If you explore a place, you travel around it to find out what it is like.

purse [pə:rs] n. 지갑; 돈, 자금; v. (입술을) 오므리다
A purse is a very small bag that people, especially women, keep their money in.

snug [snʌg] a. 꼭 맞는; 포근한, 아늑한
Something that is snug is fitting closely to your body, or fitting closely into a space.

beneath [biníːθ] prep. 아래에
Something that is beneath another thing is under the other thing.

‡ **nature** [néiʧər] n. 천성, 본성; 본질; 자연 (by nature idiom 선천적으로, 본래)
Someone's nature is their character, which they show by the way they behave.

⁎ **ladder** [lǽdər] n. 사다리
A ladder is a piece of equipment used for climbing up something or down from something.

‡ **plain** [plein] a. 보통의, 평범한; 분명한; 솔직한
If you describe someone as plain, you think they look ordinary and not at all beautiful.

⁎ **tiring** [táiəriŋ] a. 피곤하게 하는, 피곤한
If you describe something as tiring, you mean that it makes you tired so that you want to rest or sleep.

‡ **attention** [əténʃən] n. 주의 (집중), 주목; 관심, 흥미
(pay attention idiom 주의를 기울이다)
If you pay attention to someone, you watch them, listen to them, or take notice of them.

복습 **dear** [diər] n. 얘야; 여보, 당신; int. 이런!, 맙소사!; a. 사랑하는; ~에게
You can call someone dear as a sign of affection.

⁎ **roar** [rɔːr] v. (크고 깊은 소리로) 울리다; 고함치다; n. 함성; 울부짖는 듯한 소리
If something roars, it makes a very loud noise.

⁎ **launch** [lɔːnʧ] v. 발사하다; 시작하다; 맹렬히 덤비다; n. 개시; 발사
To launch a rocket, missile, or satellite means to send it into the air or into space.

⁎ **pad** [pæd] n. (우주선 등의) 발사대; 메모장; v. ~에 덧대다
A pad is a platform or an area of flat, hard ground where helicopters take off and land or rockets are launched.

‡ **gain** [gein] v. 쌓다, 늘리다; (이익·혜택을) 얻다; n. 증가; 이득
To gain something such as weight or speed means to have an increase in that particular thing.

* **soar** [sɔ:r] v. 솟구치다; (하늘 높이) 날아오르다
If something such as a bird soars into the air, it goes quickly up into the air.

복습 **farness** [fá:rnis] n. 멀리 떨어짐; 아득함
Farness is the condition of being far off.

In Space

1. **What was one thing that the Lambchops did during their first few days in space?**
   A. They gave some TV interviews.
   B. They watched many TV shows.
   C. They visited the moon.
   D. They walked around several planets.

2. **What happened on Stanley's birthday?**
   A. The Queen of England sang "Happy Birthday" to him.
   B. Stanley's classmates sang "Happy Birthday" to him.
   C. Stanley got to sing with the Westminster Boys' Choir.
   D. Stanley's friends from around the world sang "Happy Birthday" to him.

3. Why did the Lambchops suddenly lose contact with people on Earth?

   A. The President had accidentally ended the call.

   B. The Tyrrans had interrupted their connection.

   C. Some of the equipment on the spaceship had broken down.

   D. The spaceship had gone too far away from Earth.

4. What happened during the Lambchops' first radio contact with a Tyrran?

   A. The Tyrran told them to stay away from Tyrra.

   B. The Tyrran asked them if they were dangerous people.

   C. The Tyrran gave them directions to Tyrra.

   D. The Tyrran asked them what their names were.

5. What did the Lambchops realize when they reached Tyrra?

   A. They realized that the Tyrrans were in huge trouble.

   B. They realized that the Tyrrans were not really kind.

   C. They realized that the Tyrrans were quite friendly.

   D. They realized that the Tyrrans were scared of them.

Check Your Reading Speed
1분에 몇 단어를 읽는지 리딩 속도를 측정해보세요.

$$\frac{1,116 \text{ words}}{\text{reading time ( ) sec}} \times 60 = (\quad\quad) \text{ WPM}$$

Build Your Vocabulary

* **flip** [flip] v. 홱 뒤집다, 휙 젖히다; 톡 던지다; n. 톡 던지기
If something flips over, or if you flip it over or into a different position, it moves or is moved into a different position.

* **hover** [hʌvər] v. (허공을) 맴돌다; 서성이다; 주저하다; n. 공중을 떠다님
To hover means to stay in the same position in the air without moving forward or backward.

‡ **gravity** [grǽvəti] n. 중력; 심각성, 중대성; 엄숙함
Gravity is the force which causes things to drop to the ground.

‡ **force** [fɔːrs] n. 작용력; 군대; 힘; 영향력; v. ~를 강요하다; 억지로 ~하다
In physics, a force is the pulling or pushing effect that something has on something else.

* **atmosphere** [ǽtməsfìər] n. (지구의) 대기; 공기; 분위기
A planet's atmosphere is the layer of air or other gases around it.

* **clasp** [klæsp] v. 움켜쥐다; 껴안다; 잠그다; n. 걸쇠; 움켜쥐기
If you clasp someone or something, you hold them tightly in your hands or arms.

‡ **float** [flout] v. (물 위나 공중에서) 떠가다; (물에) 뜨다; n. 부표
Something that floats in or through the air hangs in it or moves slowly and gently through it.

drift [drift] v. (물·공기에) 떠가다; (서서히) 이동하다; n. 표류; 흐름
When something drifts somewhere, it is carried there by the movement of wind or water.

feather [féðər] n. (새의) 털, 깃털; v. 깃털로 덮다
A bird's feathers are the soft covering on its body.

pan [pæn] n. (손잡이가 달린 얕은) 냄비
A pan is a round metal container with a long handle, which is used for cooking things in, usually on top of a cooker or stove.

sigh [sai] v. 한숨을 쉬다, 한숨짓다; 탄식하듯 말하다; n. 한숨
When you sigh, you let out a deep breath, as a way of expressing feelings such as disappointment, tiredness, or pleasure.

adventure [ædvéntʃər] n. 모험; 모험심
If someone has an adventure, they become involved in an unusual, exciting, and rather dangerous journey or series of events.

boring [bɔ́:riŋ] a. 재미없는, 지루한
Someone or something boring is so dull and uninteresting that they make people tired and impatient.

last [læst] v. (특정한 시간 동안) 계속되다; 오래가다; ad. 맨 끝에, 마지막에
If an event, situation, or problem lasts for a particular length of time, it continues to exist or happen for that length of time.

tremendous [triméndəs] a. 엄청난; 굉장한, 대단한 (tremendously ad. 엄청나게)
You use tremendous to emphasize how strong a feeling or quality is, or how large an amount is.

magnify [mǽgnəfài] v. 확대하다; 과장하다
To magnify an object means to make it appear larger than it really is, by means of a special lens or mirror.

globe [gloub] n. 구체; 세계; 지구
Any ball-shaped object can be referred to as a globe.

‡ **steady** [stédi] a. 꾸준한; 흔들림 없는, 안정된; v. 흔들리지 않다, 진정되다
(steadily ad. 꾸준히)
A steady situation continues or develops gradually without any interruptions and is not likely to change quickly.

‡ **pale** [peil] a. (색깔이) 옅은; 창백한, 핼쑥한; v. 창백해지다
If something is pale, it is very light in color or almost white.

* **marble** [ma:rbl] n. (아이들이 가지고 노는) 구슬; 대리석
A marble is a small colored glass ball that children roll along the ground as part of a game.

‡ **sight** [sait] n. 광경, 모습; 시야; 보기, 봄; v. 갑자기 보다
A sight is something that you see.

starry [stá:ri] a. 별이 많은; 별같이 반짝이는
A starry night or sky is one in which a lot of stars are visible.

복습 **planet** [plǽnit] n. [천문] 행성
A planet is a large, round object in space that moves around a star.

‡ **broadcast** [brɔ́:dkæst] n. 방송; v. 방송하다; 널리 알리다, 광고하다
A broadcast is a program, performance, or speech on the radio or on television.

* **voyage** [vɔ́iidʒ] n. 여행, 항해; v. 여행하다, 항해하다
A voyage is a long journey on a ship or in a spacecraft.

* **release** [rilí:s] v. 공개하다; 놓아 주다; (감정을) 발산하다; n. 풀어 줌; 발표, 공개
If someone in authority releases something such as a document or information, they make it available.

복습 **press** [pres] n. 언론; 인쇄; v. 누르다; (무엇에) 바짝 대다; 꾹 밀어 넣다
Journalists are referred to as the press.

* **extraordinary** [ikstrɔ́:rdənèri] a. 보기 드문, 비범한; 기이한, 놀라운
If you describe something as extraordinary, you mean that it is very unusual or surprising.

proceed [prəsíːd] v. 진행하다; 나아가다, 이동하다
If an activity, process, or event proceeds, it goes on and does not stop.

report [ripɔ́ːrt] v. 알리다, 발표하다, 전하다; (신문·방송에서) 보도하다; n. 보도; 기록
If you report something that has happened, you tell people about it.

range [reindʒ] n. 거리, 범위; 다양성; v. 포함하다; 배열하다
The range of something is the maximum area in which it can reach things or detect things.

demonstrate [démənstrèit] v. (행동으로) 보여주다; 증거를 들어가며 보여주다
If you demonstrate a particular skill, quality, or feeling, you show by your actions that you have it.

weightless [wéitlis] a. 무게가 없는, 무중력 상태의 (weightlessness n. 무중력 상태)
A person or object is weightless when they are in space and the Earth's gravity does not affect them, so that they float around.

appreciate [əpríːʃièit] v. 고마워하다; 진가를 알아보다, 인정하다
If you appreciate something that someone has done for you or is going to do for you, you are grateful for it.

hard-pressed [haːrd-prést] a. ~을 하는 데 애를 먹는; (일·돈·시간에) 쪼들리는
If you will be hard-pressed to do something, you will have great difficulty doing it.

liven [láivən] v. 활기를 띠게 하다
To liven something means to make it more interesting or exciting.

appearance [əpíərəns] n. 출현; (겉)모습, 외모
When someone makes an appearance at a public event or in a broadcast, they take part in it.

recite [risáit] v. 암송하다, 낭송하다; 나열하다
When someone recites a poem or other piece of writing, they say it aloud after they have learned it.

poem [póuəm] n. 시

A poem is a piece of writing in which the words are chosen for their beauty and sound and are carefully arranged, often in short lines which rhyme.

bat [bæt] n. 타순; 타격; 방망이, 배트; v. (배트로) 공을 치다

(at the bat idiom 타석에 서서)

If a team or player is at the bat, it is their turn to hit the ball in baseball.

juggle [dʒʌgl] v. 저글링하다; (두 가지 이상의 일을 동시에) 하다

If you juggle, you entertain people by throwing things into the air, catching each one and throwing it up again so that there are several of them in the air at the same time.

toss [tɔːs] v. (가볍게) 던지다; (고개를) 홱 쳐들다; n. 던지기

If you toss something somewhere, you throw it there lightly, often in a rather careless way.

imitate [ímətèit] v. 흉내내다; 모방하다, 본뜨다 (imitation n. 흉내내기)

If someone does an imitation of another person, they copy the way they speak or behave, sometimes in order to be funny.

rooster [rúːstər] n. [동물] 수탉

A rooster is an adult male chicken.

stuck [stʌk] a. 갇힌; 움직일 수 없는, 꼼짝 못하는

If you are stuck in a place, you want to get away from it, but are unable to.

booth [buːθ] n. (칸막이를 한) 작은 공간; (임시) 점포 (phone booth n. (공중) 전화박스)

A booth is a small area separated from a larger public area by screens or thin walls where, for example, people can make a telephone call or vote in private.

college [kálidʒ] n. 대학(교)

A college is an institution where students study for degrees and where academic research is done.

복습 dress [dres] v. 옷을 입다; n. 드레스; 옷 (undress v. 옷을 벗다)
When you undress or undress someone, you take off your clothes or someone else's clothes.

* **accidental** [æksədéntl] a. 우연한, 돌발적인 (accidentally ad. 우연히, 뜻하지 않게)
An accidental event happens by chance or as the result of an accident, and is not deliberately intended.

mortify [mɔ́ːrtəfài] v. 굴욕감을 주다; 몹시 당황하게 하다
If you say that someone is mortified, you mean that they feel extremely offended, ashamed, or embarrassed.

* **comfort** [kʌ́mfərt] v. 위로하다, 위안하다; n. 안락, 편안; 위로, 위안
If you comfort someone, you make them feel less worried, unhappy, or upset, for example by saying kind things to them.

* **underwear** [ʌ́ndərwɛɜr] n. 속옷
Underwear is clothing such as vests and pants which you wear next to your skin under your other clothes.

복습 screen [skriːn] n. (텔레비전·컴퓨터) 화면; 칸막이; v. 가리다, 차단하다
A screen is a flat vertical surface on which pictures or words are shown.

복습 president [prézədənt] n. 대통령; 회장
The president of a country that has no king or queen is the person who is the head of state of that country.

shirtsleeve [ʃɔ́ːrtsliːv] n. 셔츠 소매
(in one's shirtsleeves idiom 셔츠 차림으로, 재킷을 입지 않고)
If a man is in shirtsleeves or in his shirtsleeves, he is wearing a shirt but not a jacket.

* **arrange** [əréindʒ] v. 마련하다, 처리하다; 정리하다, 배열하다
If you arrange an event or meeting, you make plans for it to happen.

clear one's throat idiom 목을 가다듬다; 헛기침하다
If you clear your throat, you cough once in order to make it easier to speak or to attract people's attention.

classmate [klǽsmeit] n. 급우, 반 친구
Your classmates are students who are in the same class as you at school or college.

pleased [pli:zd] a. 기쁜, 기뻐하는, 만족해하는
If you are pleased, you are happy about something or satisfied with something.

cheerful [tʃíərfəl] a. 발랄한, 쾌활한; 쾌적한 (cheerfully ad. 쾌활하게, 명랑하게)
Someone who is cheerful is happy and shows this in their behavior.

choir [kwaiər] n. 합창단, 성가대
A choir is a group of people who sing together, for example in a church or school.

attention [əténʃən] n. 주의 (집중), 주목; 관심, 흥미
If you give someone or something your attention, you look at it, listen to it, or think about it carefully.

jealous [dʒéləs] a. 질투하는; 시샘하는
If you are jealous of another person's possessions or qualities, you feel angry or bitter because you do not have them.

entertain [èntərtéin] v. 즐겁게 해 주다; (집에서 손님을) 접대하다
If a performer, performance, or activity entertains you, it amuses you, interests you, or gives you pleasure.

tease [ti:z] n. 장난, 놀림; v. 놀리다, 장난하다; (동물을) 못 살게 굴다
A tease is something that someone says or does when they are laughing at you in order to embarrass or annoy you.

fellow [félou] n. 녀석, 친구; 동료; a. 동료의
A fellow is a man or boy.

amuse [əmjú:z] v. 즐겁게 하다, 재미있게 하다 (amused a. 재미있어하는)
If you are amused by something, it makes you want to laugh or smile.

cheer [tʃiər] v. 기운이 나다; 환호성을 지르다, 환호하다; n. 환호(성), 응원의 함성
If you are cheered by something, it makes you happier or less worried.

44

blank [blæŋk] a. 빈; 멍한, 무표정한; n. 빈칸, 여백; v. (갑자기) 멍해지다
Something that is blank has nothing on it.

sail [seil] v. 항해하다; 미끄러지듯 나아가다; n. 돛
If you sail a boat or if a boat sails, it moves across water using its sails.

board [bɔːrd] n. 판; 이사회; v. 승선하다, 탑승하다
A board is a square piece of wood or stiff cardboard that you use for playing games such as chess.

greeting [gríːtiŋ] int. (pl.) 안녕하십니까; n. 인사
'Greetings' is an old-fashioned way of saying hello to someone.

mighty [máiti] a. 강력한, 힘센; ad. 대단히, 굉장히
Mighty is used to describe something that is very large or powerful.

sake [seik] n. (~을) 위함 (for heaven's sake idiom 제발, 부디, 맙소사)
Some people use expressions such as 'for heaven's sake' or 'for God's sake' in order to express annoyance or impatience, or to add force to a question or request.

party [páːrti] n. 일행; 파티; 정당
A party of people is a group of people who are doing something together, for example travelling together.

tail [teil] n. 끝부분; (동물의) 꼬리; v. 미행하다
You can use tail to refer to the end or back of something, especially something long and thin.

formation [fɔːrméiʃən] n. 형태; (특정한) 대형, 편대; 형성
A rock or cloud formation is rock or cloud of a particular shape or structure.

lopsided [lapsáidid] a. 한쪽이 처진, 한쪽으로 치우친
Something that is lopsided is uneven because one side is lower or heavier than the other.

pointy [pɔ́inti] a. 끝이 뾰족한; 가시가 돋은
Something that is pointy has a point at one end.

✦✦ field [fiːld] n. 들판, 밭; ~장; 분야; 현장
A field is an area of grass, for example in a park or on a farm.

✦✦ land [lænd] v. (땅·표면에) 내려앉다, 착륙하다; (땅에) 떨어지다; n. 육지, 땅; 지역
When someone lands a plane, ship, or spacecraft, or when it lands, it arrives somewhere after a journey.

복습 bet [bet] v. ~이 틀림없다; (내기 등에) 돈을 걸다; n. 내기; 짐작, 추측
You use 'you bet' to say yes in an emphatic way or to emphasize a reply or statement.

✦ contact [kántækt] n. 연락, 접촉; v. (전화·편지 등으로) 연락하다
Contact involves meeting or communicating with someone, especially regularly.

복습 vanish [vǽniʃ] v. 사라지다, 없어지다; 모습을 감추다
If someone or something vanishes, they disappear suddenly or in a way that cannot be explained.

✦ descend [disénd] v. 내려오다, 내려가다; (아래로) 경사지다
If you descend or if you descend a staircase, you move downward from a higher to a lower level.

복습 reach [riːʧ] v. ~에 이르다; (손·팔을) 뻗다; n. (닿을 수 있는) 거리; 범위
When someone or something reaches a place, they arrive there.

복습 shade [ʃeid] n. 색조; 창문 블라인드; 그늘; v. 그늘지게 하다, (빛을) 가리다
A shade of a particular color is one of its different forms.

marking [máːrkiŋ] n. 표시; 무늬
Markings are colored lines, shapes, or patterns on the surface of something, which help to identify it.

✦ continent [kántənənt] n. 대륙; 육지
A continent is a very large area of land, such as Africa or Asia, that consists of several countries.

touch down idiom (비행기·우주선 등이) 착륙하다
If an aircraft or space vehicle touches down, it comes down to the ground.

peer [piər] v. 유심히 보다, 눈여겨보다; n. 또래
If you peer at something, you look at it very hard, usually because it is difficult to see clearly.

brownish [bráuniʃ] a. 약간 갈색인, 갈색을 띠는
Something that is brownish is slightly brown in color.

curious [kjúəriəs] a. 별난, 특이한; 궁금한, 호기심이 많은
If you describe something as curious, you mean that it is unusual or difficult to understand.

expect [ikspékt] v. 예상하다, 기대하다
If you expect something to happen, you believe that it will happen.

surrender [səréndər] v. 항복하다, 투항하다; (권리 등을) 포기하다; n. 항복, 굴복
If you surrender, you stop fighting or resisting someone and agree that you have been beaten.

trap [træp] v. (함정으로) 몰아넣다; (위험한 장소·궁지에) 가두다; n. 덫, 올가미; 함정
If you are trapped somewhere, something falls onto you or blocks your way and prevents you from moving or escaping.

breakable [bréikəbl] a. 깨지기 쉬운 (unbreakable a. 부서뜨릴 수 없는)
Unbreakable objects cannot be broken, usually because they are made of a very strong material.

cable [keibl] n. 굵은 철제 밧줄; 전선, 케이블
A cable is a kind of very strong, thick rope, made of wires twisted together.

prisoner [prízənər] n. 포로, 죄수
A prisoner is a person who has been captured by an enemy, for example in war.

The Tyrrans

1. **What happened when Stanley turned on the window wiper?**

   A. The window became cleaner.

   B. The Tyrrans quickly surrendered.

   C. A tyrran came running toward the *Star Scout*.

   D. The unbreakable trapping cable broke.

2. **What did a messenger look like?**

   A. He had a friendly smile.

   B. He looked old.

   C. He looked tiny.

   D. He had a small mustache.

3. What did the messenger think before he actually saw the Lambchops?

A. He thought Tyrrans were nicer than people from Earth.

B. He thought people from Earth were smarter than Tyrrans.

C. He thought people from Earth were smaller than Tyrrans.

D. He thought people from Earth were bigger than Tyrrans.

4. Who was NOT a part of the Tyrran truce committee?

A. The scientist of Tyrra

B. The Captain of the Tyrran spaceship

C. The Commander of the Tyrran forces

D. The President of Tyrra

5. Why did the Lambchops carry magnifying lenses to TyrraVille?

A. They needed the magnifying lenses in order to see the Tyrran committee and look around TyrraVille.

B. The Tyrran committee had asked them to show the magnifying lenses to its people.

C. The magnifying lenses would help guide them back to the spaceship later.

D. They could use the magnifying lenses as a weapon if necessary.

Check Your Reading Speed

1분에 몇 단어를 읽는지 리딩 속도를 측정해보세요.

$$\frac{792 \text{ words}}{\text{reading time ( ) sec}} \times 60 = (\quad) \text{ WPM}$$

Build Your Vocabulary

^{복습} **breakable** [bréikəbl] a. 깨지기 쉬운 (unbreakable a. 부서뜨릴 수 없는)
Unbreakable objects cannot be broken, usually because they are made of a very strong material.

^{복습} **trap** [træp] v. (함정으로) 몰아넣다; (위험한 장소·궁지에) 가두다; n. 덫, 올가미; 함정
If you are trapped somewhere, something falls onto you or blocks your way and prevents you from moving or escaping.

^{복습} **cable** [keibl] n. 굵은 철제 밧줄; 전선, 케이블
A cable is a kind of very strong, thick rope, made of wires twisted together.

^{복습} **prisoner** [prízənər] n. 포로, 죄수
A prisoner is a person who has been captured by an enemy, for example in war.

^{복습} **surrender** [səréndər] v. 항복하다, 투항하다; (권리 등을) 포기하다; n. 항복, 굴복
If you surrender, you stop fighting or resisting someone and agree that you have been beaten.

* **scarcely** [skéərsli] ad. 거의 ~않다; 겨우, 간신히
You use scarcely to emphasize that something is only just true or only just the case.

^{복습} **peaceful** [pí:sfəl] a. 평화적인; 평화로운
Peaceful people are not violent and try to avoid quarrelling or fighting with other people.

mislead [mìslíːd] v. (misled–misled) 나쁜 일에 꾀어들이다, 속이다
If you say that someone has misled you, you mean that they have made you believe something which is not true, either by telling you a lie or by giving you a wrong idea or impression.

seaside [síːsaid] n. (휴가 등을 위해 찾는) 해변
You can refer to an area that is close to the sea, especially one where people go for their holidays, as the seaside.

thin [θin] a. 얇은, 가는; 마른
Something that is thin is much narrower than it is long.

thread [θred] n. 실; 가느다란 줄기; v. (실 등을) 꿰다
Thread or a thread is a long very thin piece of a material such as cotton, nylon, or silk, especially one that is used in sewing.

scout [skaut] n. 정찰병; 스카우트; v. (무엇을 찾아) 돌아다니다; 정찰하다
A scout is someone who is sent to an area of countryside to find out the position of an enemy army.

switch on idiom (전등 등의) 스위치를 켜다
If you switch on something such as an electrical device, a machine, or an engine, you start it working by pressing a switch or a button.

wiper [wáipər] n. (자동차 앞 유리의) 와이퍼
A wiper is a device that wipes rain from a vehicle's windscreen.

flick [flik] n. 재빨리 움직임; v. 튀기다, 털다; 잽싸게 움직이다
A flick means a sudden quick movement.

blade [bleid] n. (칼·도구 등의) 날
The blade of a knife, ax, or saw is the edge, which is used for cutting.

part [paːrt] v. (사물이) 갈라지다, 나뉘다; (사람과 사람을) 갈라놓다
If things that are next to each other part or if you part them, they move in opposite directions, so that there is a space between them.

startle [stɑ:rtl] v. 깜짝 놀라게 하다; 움찔하다; n. 깜짝 놀람
If something sudden and unexpected startles you, it surprises and frightens you slightly.

messenger [mésəndʒər] n. 전달자, 배달원
A messenger takes a message to someone, or takes messages regularly as their job.

ordinary [ɔ́:rdənèri] a. 보통의, 평범한
Ordinary people or things are normal and not special or different in any way.

keep one's eye on idiom ~에서 눈을 떼지 않다; 경계하다
If you keep your eyes on someone or something, you are watching them carefully and closely.

field [fi:ld] n. 들판, 밭; ~장; 분야; 현장
A field is an area of grass, for example in a park or on a farm.

trail away idiom (목소리가) 차츰 잦아들다
If a speaker's voice or a speaker trails away, their voice becomes quieter and they hesitate until they stop speaking completely.

muscular [mʌ́skjulur] a. 근육질의; 근육의
If a person or their body is muscular, they are very fit and strong, and have firm muscles which are not covered with a lot of fat.

scowl [skaul] v. 노려보다, 쏘아보다; n. 노려봄, 쏘아봄
When someone scowls, an angry or hostile expression appears on their face.

curl [kə:rl] v. 돌돌 감기다; 곱슬곱슬하다; (몸을) 웅크리다; n. 곱슬곱슬한 머리카락
If something curls somewhere, or if you curl it there, it moves there in a spiral or curve.

mustache [mʌ́stæʃ] n. 콧수염
A man's mustache is the hair that grows on his upper lip.

‡ **club** [klʌb] n. 곤봉; 클럽, 동호회; v. (곤봉 같은 것으로) 때리다
A club is a thick heavy stick that can be used as a weapon.

‡ **crack** [kræk] n. (좁은) 틈; (갈라져 생긴) 금; v. 깨뜨리다, 부수다; 갈라지다, 금이 가다
If you open something such as a door, window, or curtain a crack, you open it only a small amount.

⋆ **enormous** [inɔ́:rməs] a. 막대한, 거대한
Something that is enormous is extremely large in size or amount.

‡ **fling** [fliŋ] v. (거칠게) 내던지다; (머리·팔 등을) 휘두르다; n. 내던지기, 팽개치기
If you fling something into a particular place or position, you put it there in a quick or angry way.

복습 **rest** [rest] n. 나머지; 휴식; v. 쉬다; 놓이다, (~에) 있다
The rest is used to refer to all the parts of something or all the things in a group that remain or that you have not already mentioned.

복습 **tease** [ti:z] v. 놀리다, 장난하다; (동물을) 못 살게 굴다; n. 장난, 놀림
To tease someone means to laugh at them or make jokes about them in order to embarrass, annoy, or upset them.

⋆ **faint** [feint] v. 실신하다, 기절하다; n. 실신, 기절; a. 희미한, 약한
If you faint, you lose consciousness for a short time, especially because you are hungry, or because of pain, heat, or shock.

‡ **handkerchief** [hǽŋkərʧif] n. 손수건
A handkerchief is a small square piece of fabric which you use for blowing your nose.

dab [dæb] v. (가볍게) 누르다; 살짝 바르다; n. (가볍게) 꼭꼭 누르기
If you dab something, you touch it several times using quick, light movements.

‡ **tiny** [táini] a. 아주 작은
Something or someone that is tiny is extremely small.

⋆ **brow** [brau] n. 이마; (pl.) 눈썹
Your brow is your forehead.

^복^습spaceship [spéisʃip] n. 우주선
A spaceship is a rocket or other vehicle that carries people through space.

· gross [grous] a. 역겨운; 아주 무례한; ad. 모두 (합해서)
If you describe something as gross, you think it is very unpleasant.

· grasp [græsp] v. 꽉 잡다; 완전히 이해하다; n. 통제; 움켜잡기; 이해
If you grasp something, you take it in your hand and hold it very firmly.

· furious [fjúəriəs] a. 몹시 화가 난; 맹렬한
Someone who is furious is extremely angry.

⁕ · swing [swiŋ] v. (swung–swung) 휘두르다; (전후 · 좌우로) 흔들다; 휙 움직이다;
n. 흔들기; 휘두르기
If something swings or if you swing it, it moves repeatedly backward
and forward or from side to side from a fixed point.

· tap [tæp] v. (가볍게) 톡톡 두드리다; 이용하다; n. (가볍게) 두드리기
If you tap something, you hit it with a quick light blow or a series of
quick light blows.

· ouch [autʃ] int. 아야 (갑자기 아파서 내지르는 소리)
'Ouch!' is used in writing to represent the noise that people make when
they suddenly feel pain.

scat [skæt] int. 저리 가라!
'Scat!' is said to an animal, especially a cat, or to a person to make them
go away quickly.

· dart [da:rt] v. 쏜살같이 움직이다; 흘깃 쳐다보다; n. (작은) 화살; 쏜살같이 달림
If a person or animal darts somewhere, they move there suddenly and
quickly.

never mind idiom 신경 쓰지 마
You use never mind to tell someone that they need not do something
or worry about something, because it is not important or because you
will do it yourself.

truce [tru:s] n. 휴전
A truce is an agreement between two people or groups of people to stop fighting or quarrelling for a short time.

committee [kəmíti] n. 위원회
A committee is a group of people who meet to make decisions or plans for a larger group or organization that they represent.

flag [flæg] n. 기, 깃발; v. 표시를 하다; 지치다; 약해지다
A flag is a piece of cloth which can be attached to a pole and which is used as a sign, signal, or symbol of something, especially of a particular country.

flutter [flʌ́tər] v. (가볍게) 펄럭이다; 흔들다; n. 흔들림
If something thin or light flutters, or if you flutter it, it moves up and down or from side to side with a lot of quick, light movements.

make out idiom ~을 알아보다; 주장하다
If you make someone or something out, you see, hear, or understand them with difficulty.

uniform [júːnəfɔ̀ːrm] n. 제복, 군복, 유니폼 (uniformed a. 제복을 입은)
A uniform is a special set of clothes which some people, for example soldiers or the police, wear to work in and which some children wear at school.

stout [staut] a. 통통한; 튼튼한
A stout person is rather fat.

suit [suːt] n. 정장; (특정한 활동 때 입는) 옷; v. 어울리다; ~에게 편리하다
A man's suit consists of a jacket, trousers, and sometimes a waistcoat, all made from the same fabric.

wavy [wéivi] a. 웨이브가 있는, 물결 모양의
Wavy hair is not straight or curly, but curves slightly.

bald [bɔːld] a. 대머리의, 머리가 벗겨진
Someone who is bald has little or no hair on the top of their head.

⋆ halt [hɔːlt] v. 멈추다, 서다; 중단시키다; n. 멈춤, 중단
When a person or a vehicle halts or when something halts them, they stop moving in the direction they were going and stand still.

⋆ stare [stɛər] v. 빤히 쳐다보다, 응시하다; n. 빤히 쳐다보기, 응시
If you stare at someone or something, you look at them for a long time.

⋆ commander [kəmǽndər] n. 지휘관, 사령관
A commander is an officer in charge of a military operation or organization.

복습 force [fɔːrs] n. 군대; 작용력; 힘; 영향력; v. ~를 강요하다; 억지로 ~하다
Forces are groups of soldiers or military vehicles that are organized for a particular purpose.

복습 chief [ʧiːf] a. (계급·직급상) 최고위자인; n. (조직·집단의) 장(長)
Chief is used in the job titles of the most senior worker or workers of a particular kind in an organization.

복습 pilot [páilət] n. 조종사, 비행사
A pilot is a person who is trained to fly an aircraft.

⋆ indicate [índikèit] v. (손가락이나 고갯짓으로) 가리키다; 나타내다, 보여 주다
If you indicate something to someone, you show them where it is, especially by pointing to it.

⋆ chap [ʧæp] n. 녀석, 친구
A chap is a man or boy.

grouchy [gráuʧi] a. 불평이 많은, 잘 투덜거리는
If someone is grouchy, they are very bad-tempered and complain a lot.

⋆ aide [eid] n. 부관; 보좌관
An aide is an assistant to someone who has an important job, especially in government or in the armed forces.

복복 polite [pəláit] a. 예의상의, 의례적인; 공손한, 정중한
Someone who is polite has good manners and behaves in a way that is socially correct and not rude to other people.

remark [rimá:rk] n. 말, 발언; 주목; v. 언급하다, 말하다
If you make a remark about something, you say something about it.

realize [rí:əlàiz] v. 깨닫다, 알아차리다; 실현하다
If you realize that something is true, you become aware of that fact or understand it.

knee [ni:] n. 무릎; v. 무릎으로 치다 (get down on one's kness idiom 무릎을 꿇다)
Your knee is the place where your leg bends.

follow one's example idiom (행동·태도 등을) 따라하다
If you follow someone's example, you behave in the same way as they did in the past, or in a similar way, especially because you admire them.

at once idiom 즉시; 동시에
If you do something at once, you do it immediately.

lower [lóuər] v. ~을 내리다; 낮추다
If you lower something, you move it slowly downward.

relieve [rilí:v] v. 안도하게 하다; (불쾌감·고통 등을) 없애 주다; 완화하다
(relief n. 안도, 안심)
If you feel a sense of relief, you feel happy because something unpleasant has not happened or is no longer happening.

reasonable [rí:zənəbl] a. 합리적인; 타당한; 상당히 괜찮은
If you think that someone is fair and sensible you can say that they are reasonable.

frankly [frǽŋkli] ad. 솔직히, 솔직히 말하면
You use frankly when you are expressing an opinion or feeling to emphasize that you mean what you are saying, especially when the person you are speaking to may not like it.

growl [graul] v. 으르렁거리듯 말하다; 으르렁거리다; n. 으르렁거리는 소리
If someone growls something, they say something in a low, rough, and angry voice.

sniff [snif] v. 콧방귀를 뀌다; 냄새를 맡다; 코를 훌쩍이다; n. 냄새 맡기; 콧방귀 뀌기
You can use sniff to indicate that someone says something in a way that shows their disapproval or contempt.

frighten [fraitn] v. 겁먹게 하다, 놀라게 하다
If something or someone frightens you, they cause you to suddenly feel afraid, anxious, or nervous.

petite [pətíːt] a. 자그마한
If you describe a woman as petite, you are politely saying that she is small and is not fat.

scare [skɛər] v. 겁주다, 놀라게 하다; 무서워하다; n. 불안(감); 놀람, 공포
If something scares you, it frightens or worries you.

harm [haːrm] n. 해, 피해, 손해; v. 해치다; 손상시키다
(no harm done idiom (큰 피해가 아니니) 괜찮다)
If you say that there is no harm done, you are telling someone not to worry about something that has happened because it has not caused any serious injury or damage.

capital [kǽpətl] n. 수도; 자본금, 자금; 자산; a. 대문자의
The capital of a country is the city or town where its government or parliament meets.

stroll [stroul] n. (한가로이) 거닐기, 산책; v. 거닐다, 산책하다
A stroll refers to an act of walking, especially for pleasure.

equip [ikwíp] v. 장비를 갖추다; (지식 등을 가르쳐) 준비를 갖춰 주다
If you equip a person or thing with something, you give them the tools or equipment that are needed.

handy [hǽndi] a. 유용한, 편리한
Something that is handy is useful.

kit [kit] n. (도구·장비) 세트; 조립용품 세트
A kit is a group of items that are kept together, often in the same container, because they are all used for similar purposes.

★ **court** [kɔːrt] n. (테니스) 코트; 법정, 법원

A court is an area in which you play a game such as tennis, basketball, badminton, or squash.

TyrraVille

1. What was TyrraVille like?

A. It was quiet and empty.

B. It looked similar to a small village on Earth.

C. It had lots of trees and grass.

D. It seemed very disorganized because there were so many people.

2. How did the Tyrran people react when they saw the Lambchops?

A. They were unimpressed by the Lambchops.

B. They were relieved to meet the Lambchops.

C. They avoided going near the Lambchops.

D. They greeted the Lambchops in a kind way.

3. Why did Captain Ik want to use the Magno-Titanic Paralyzer Ray on the Lambchops?

   A. He wanted to help the Tyrran people.

   B. He wanted to make sure the machine worked.

   C. He wanted to frighten the Lambchops.

   D. He wanted to take over the Lambchops' spaceship.

4. Why did the Magno-Titanic beam hit Stanley?

   A. Captain Ik had wanted to paralyze Stanley first.

   B. Captain Ik couldn't control the machine well.

   C. Stanley had stepped in front of Arthur to protect him.

   D. Stanley was the only person standing nearby.

5. Why wasn't Stanley paralyzed by the beam?

   A. The Magno-Titanic machine was fake.

   B. The beam couldn't work well in the rain.

   C. Stanley was not close enough to the beam to be paralyzed.

   D. Stanley was too big to be affected by the beam.

Check Your Reading Speed

1분에 몇 단어를 읽는지 리딩 속도를 측정해보세요.

$$\frac{677 \ words}{reading \ time \ (\quad) \ sec} \times 60 = (\quad) \ WPM$$

Build Your Vocabulary

gosh [gaʃ] int. (놀람·기쁨을 나타내어) 어머!, 뭐라고!
Some people say 'Gosh' when they are surprised.

homesick [hóumsik] a. 고향을 그리워하는, 향수병을 앓는
If you are homesick, you feel unhappy because you are away from home and are missing your family, friends, and home very much.

except [iksépt] prep. ~을 제외하고는
You use except for to introduce the only thing or person that prevents a statement from being completely true.

lack [læk] n. 부족, 결핍; v. ~이 없다, 부족하다
If there is a lack of something, there is not enough of it or it does not exist at all.

capital [kǽpətl] n. 수도; 자본금, 자금; 자산; a. 대문자의
The capital of a country is the city or town where its government or parliament meets.

bustle [bʌsl] v. 바삐 움직이다, 서두르다; n. 부산함, 북적거림
A place that is bustling with people or activity is full of people who are very busy or lively.

errand [érənd] n. 볼일; 심부름 (run an errand idiom 볼일을 보다)
If you run an errand, you do or get something, usually by making a short trip somewhere.

spire [spaiər] n. 첨탑; v. 돌출하다, 쑥 내밀다
The spire of a building such as a church is the tall pointed structure on the top.

waist [weist] n. 허리
Your waist is the middle part of your body where it narrows slightly above your hips.

side street [sáid striːt] n. 골목, 옆길
A side street is a quiet, often narrow street which leads off a busier street.

lawn [lɔːn] n. 잔디밭, 잔디
A lawn is an area of grass that is kept cut short and is usually part of someone's garden or backyard, or part of a park.

neat [niːt] a. 아기자기한; 정돈된, 단정한
A neat object, part of the body, or shape is quite small and has a smooth outline.

postage stamp [póustidʒ stæmp] n. 우표
A postage stamp is a small piece of gummed paper that you buy from the post office and stick on an envelope or package before you post it.

march [maːrʧ] v. (단호한 태도로 급히) 걸어가다; 행진하다; n. 행군, 행진; 3월
If you say that someone marches somewhere, you mean that they walk there quickly and in a determined way, for example because they are angry.

rest [rest] n. 나머지; 휴식; v. 쉬다; 놓이다, (~에) 있다
The rest is used to refer to all the parts of something or all the things in a group that remain or that you have not already mentioned.

committee [kəmíti] n. 위원회
A committee is a group of people who meet to make decisions or plans for a larger group or organization that they represent.

halt [hɔːlt] v. 멈추다, 서다; 중단시키다; n. 멈춤, 중단
When a person or a vehicle halts or when something halts them, they stop moving in the direction they were going and stand still.

president [prézədənt] n. 대통령; 회장
The president of a country that has no king or queen is the person who is the head of state of that country.

risk [risk] n. 위험; 위험 요소; v. 위태롭게 하다; 과감히 ～을 하다
If there is a risk of something unpleasant, there is a possibility that it will happen.

scarcely [skéərsli] ad. 거의 ～않다; 겨우, 간신히
You use scarcely to emphasize that something is only just true or only just the case.

escort [ésko:rt] v. ～을 바래다주다; 호송하다, 호위하다; n. 호위대
If you escort someone somewhere, you accompany them there, usually in order to make sure that they leave a place or get to their destination.

circle [sə:rkl] v. 에워싸다, 둘러싸다; 빙빙 돌다; n. 원형
To circle around someone or something, or to circle them, means to move around them.

bend [bend] v. (몸·머리를) 굽히다, 숙이다; 구부리다; n. (도로·강의) 굽이, 굽은 곳
When you bend, you move the top part of your body downward and forward.

magnify [mǽgnəfài] v. 확대하다; 과장하다
To magnify an object means to make it appear larger than it really is, by means of a special lens or mirror.

take care idiom ～을 처리하다; ～을 돌보다
If you take care to do something, you make sure that you do it.

indicate [índikèit] v. (손가락이나 고갯짓으로) 가리키다; 나타내다, 보여 주다
If you indicate something to someone, you show them where it is, especially by pointing to it.

particular [pərtíkjulər] a. 특별한; 특정한; 까다로운; n. 자세한 사실
You can use particular to emphasize that something is greater or more intense than usual.

⁑ square [skwɛər] n. 광장; 정사각형; a. 정사각형 모양의; 직각의; 공정한
In a town or city, a square is a flat open place, often in the shape of a square.

⁎ whisper [hwíspər] v. 속삭이다, 소곤거리다; n. 속삭임, 소곤거리는 소리
When you whisper, you say something very quietly, using your breath rather than your throat, so that only one person can hear you.

복습 stir [stəːr] n. 동요, 충격; 젓기; v. 젓다, (저어 가며) 섞다; 약간 움직이다
If an event causes a stir, it causes great excitement, shock, or anger among people.

복습 tiny [táini] a. 아주 작은
Something or someone that is tiny is extremely small.

⁎ citizen [sítəzən] n. 주민, 시민
Someone who is a citizen of a particular country is legally accepted as belonging to that country.

⁎ wave [weiv] v. (손·팔을) 흔들다; 흔들리다; n. 파도, 물결; (손·팔을) 흔들기
If you wave or wave your hand, you move your hand from side to side in the air, usually in order to say hello or goodbye to someone.

⁎ roof [ruːf] n. 지붕; v. 지붕을 씌우다 (rooftop n. 옥상)
A rooftop is the outside part of the roof of a building.

⁎ journalist [dʒə́ːrnəlist] n. 기자
A journalist is a person whose job is to collect news and write about it for newspapers, magazines, television, or radio.

⁑ treat [triːt] v. 대접하다; (특정한 태도로) 대하다; 치료하다; n. (대접하는) 특별한 것; 기쁨
If you treat someone to something special which they will enjoy, you buy it or arrange it for them.

⁎ tub [tʌb] n. 통; 욕조
A tub is a deep container of any size.

⁎ portion [pɔ́ːrʃən] n. 1인분; 부분; v. 분배하다
A portion is the amount of food that is given to one person at a meal.

refresh [rifréʃ] v. 생기를 되찾게 하다; ~의 기억을 새롭게 하다
If something refreshes you when you have become hot, tired, or thirsty, it makes you feel cooler or more energetic.

hurdle [hə:rdl] v. ~을 뛰어넘다; n. (경기용) 허들; 장애, 난관
If you hurdle, you jump over something while you are running.

land [lænd] v. (땅·표면에) 내려앉다, 착륙하다; (땅에) 떨어지다; n. 육지, 땅; 지역
When someone or something lands, they come down to the ground after moving through the air or falling.

scold [skould] v. 야단치다, 꾸짖다
If you scold someone, you speak angrily to them because they have done something wrong.

look on idiom (관여하지는 않고) 구경하다
To look on means to watch an event or an incident without taking part in it yourself.

tug [tʌg] v. (세게) 잡아당기다; n. (갑자기 세게) 잡아당김
If you tug something or tug at it, you give it a quick and usually strong pull.

address [ədrés] v. 말을 걸다; 연설하다; 주소를 쓰다; n. 주소; 연설
If you address someone or address a remark to them, you say something to them.

squint [skwint] v. 눈을 가늘게 뜨고 보다; 사시이다; n. 사시; 잠깐 봄
If you squint at something, you look at it with your eyes partly closed.

hardly [há:rdli] ad. 거의 ~할 수가 없다; 거의 ~아니다; ~하자마자
When you say you can hardly do something, you are emphasizing that it is very difficult for you to do it.

dot [dat] n. 점같이 작은 것; 점; v. 여기저기 흩어져 있다, 산재하다; 점을 찍다
You can refer to something that you can see in the distance and that looks like a small round mark as a dot.

make fun of idiom ~을 놀리다, 비웃다
If you make fun of someone or something, you laugh at them, tease them, or make jokes about them in a way that causes them to seem ridiculous.

exclaim [ikskléim] v. 소리치다, 외치다
If you exclaim, you cry out suddenly in surprise, strong emotion, or pain.

surrender [səréndər] v. 항복하다, 투항하다; (권리 등을) 포기하다; n. 항복, 굴복
If you surrender, you stop fighting or resisting someone and agree that you have been beaten.

stagger [stǽgər] v. 비틀거리다, 휘청거리다; 큰 충격을 주다
If you stagger, you walk very unsteadily, for example because you are ill or drunk.

beneath [biníːθ] prep. 아래에
Something that is beneath another thing is under the other thing.

weight [weit] n. 무거운 것; 무게, 체중
You can refer to a heavy object as a weight, especially when you have to lift it.

tube [tjuːb] n. 관; 튜브; 통
A tube is a long hollow object that is usually round, like a pipe.

stick out idiom (툭) 튀어나오다, ~을 내밀다
If something is sticking out from a surface or object, it extends up or away from it.

resist [rizíst] v. 저항하다; 굴하지 않다; 참다, 견디다
If you resist someone or resist an attack by them, you fight back against them.

paralyze [pǽrəlàiz] v. 마비시키다; 무력하게 하다; 쓸모없게 하다
If someone is paralyzed by an accident or an illness, they have no feeling in their body, or in part of their body, and are unable to move.

⋆ ray [rei] n. 광선; 약간, 소량
Rays of light are narrow beams of light.

복습 truce [truːs] n. 휴전
A truce is an agreement between two people or groups of people to stop fighting or quarrelling for a short time.

⋆ bark [baːrk] v. (명령·질문 등을) 빽 내지르다; (개가) 짖다; n. 나무껍질; (개 등이) 짖는 소리
If you bark at someone, you shout at them aggressively in a loud, rough voice.

복습 knee [niː] n. 무릎; v. 무릎으로 치다
Your knee is the place where your leg bends.

⋆ buckle [bʌkl] v. (다리의 힘이) 풀리다; 찌그러지다; 버클로 잠그다; n. 버클
If your legs or knees buckle, they bend because they have become very weak or tired.

⋆ recover [rikʌ́vər] v. (의식 등을) 되찾다; 회복되다; (손실 등을) 되찾다
If you recover a mental or physical state, it comes back again.

복습 scare [skɛər] v. 겁주다, 놀라게 하다; 무서워하다; n. 불안(감); 놀람, 공포
If something scares you, it frightens or worries you.

flicker [flíkər] v. (불·빛 등이) 깜박거리다; 움직거리다; n. (빛의) 깜박거림; 움직거림
If a light or flame flickers, it shines unsteadily.

yikes [jaiks] int. 어이구, 어어 (놀라거나 무서울 때 내는 소리)
You can say 'yikes' as an expression of surprise, fear, or alarm.

⋆ shriek [ʃriːk] n. 비명; v. (날카롭게) 비명을 지르다; 악을 쓰며 말하다
A shriek is a loud, high sound made because you are frightened, excited, or angry.

복습 crowd [kraud] n. 사람들, 군중; v. 가득 메우다; (생각이 마음속에) 밀려오다
A crowd is a large group of people who have gathered together.

＊beam [biːm] n. 빛줄기; 기둥; v. 활짝 웃다; 비추다
A beam is a line of energy, radiation, or particles sent in a particular direction.

＊spring [spriŋ] v. (sprung/sprang–sprung) 휙 움직이다, (갑자기) 뛰어오르다; (~의) 출신이다; n. 봄; 생기, 활기; 샘
When a person or animal springs, they jump upward or forward suddenly or quickly.

＊protect [prətékt] v. 보호하다, 지키다; 보장하다
To protect someone or something means to prevent them from being harmed or damaged.

＊faint [feint] v. 실신하다, 기절하다; n. 실신, 기절; a. 희미한, 약한
If you faint, you lose consciousness for a short time, especially because you are hungry, or because of pain, heat, or shock.

＊fright [frait] n. 놀람, 두려움
Fright is a sudden feeling of fear, especially the fear that you feel when something unpleasant surprises you.

＊roll [roul] v. (다른 쪽으로) 돌다; 굴리다; (빙글빙글) 돌다; n. 두루마리; 뒹굴기
When something rolls or when you roll it, it moves along a surface, turning over many times.

wiggle [wigl] v. 꼼틀꼼틀 움직이다; n. 꼼틀꼼틀 움직이기
If you wiggle something or if it wiggles, it moves up and down or from side to side in small quick movements.

hoot [huːt] v. 시끄럽게 떠들어대다; 폭소를 터뜨리다; n. 폭소; 비웃음
If you hoot, you make a loud high-pitched noise when you are laughing or showing disapproval.

ninny [níni] n. 멍청이
If you refer to someone as a ninny, you think that they are foolish or silly.

＊drift [drift] v. (서서히) 이동하다; (물·공기에) 떠가다; n. 표류; 흐름
To drift somewhere means to move there slowly or gradually.

stern [stəːrn] a. 엄중한, 근엄한; 심각한 (sternly ad. 엄격하게, 준엄하게)
Someone who is stern is very serious and strict.

pray [prei] ad. 제발, 정말; v. 간절히 바라다; 기도하다, 빌다
Pray is used for asking a question or for telling someone to do something.

attempt [ətémpt] v. 시도하다, 애써 해보다; n. 시도
If you attempt to do something, especially something difficult, you try to do it.

glance [glæns] n. 흘낏 봄; v. 흘낏 보다; 대충 훑어보다
A glance is a quick look at someone or something.

stare [stɛər] v. 빤히 쳐다보다, 응시하다; n. 빤히 쳐다보기, 응시
If you stare at someone or something, you look at them for a long time.

crisis [kráisis] n. 위기; 최악의 고비
A crisis is a situation in which something or someone is affected by one or more very serious problems.

burst [bəːrst] v. (burst–burst) 갑자기 ~하다; 터지다, 파열하다; 불쑥 움직이다; n. (갑자기) 한바탕 ~을 함
To burst into something means to suddenly start doing it.

sake [seik] n. (~을) 위함 (for heaven's sake idiom 제발, 부디, 맙소사)
Some people use expressions such as 'for heaven's sake' or 'for God's sake' in order to express annoyance or impatience, or to add force to a question or request.

puzzle [pʌzl] v. 어리둥절하게 하다; n. 퍼즐; 수수께끼
(puzzled a. 어리둥절해하는, 얼떨떨한)
Someone who is puzzled is confused because they do not understand something.

darken [dáːrkən] v. 어두워지다; 우울해지다
If something darkens or if a person or thing darkens it, it becomes darker.

★ **shelter** [ʃéltər] n. 대피처, 피신처; 피신; v. 막아 주다, 보호하다; 피하다
A shelter is a small building or covered place which is made to protect people from bad weather or danger.

President Ot's Story

1. What crisis is Tyrra facing?

   A. The planet is being threatened by enemies.

   B. The planet is running out of Fizzola.

   C. The planet does not have any more fresh food or water.

   D. The planet does not have enough money for its inventions.

2. What was one thing that Super-Gro was supposed to do?

   A. It was supposed to make crops bigger.

   B. It was supposed to make bottles safer.

   C. It was supposed to make food healthier.

   D. It was supposed to make grass greener.

3. What happened after the Super-Gro exploded and the rain came?

   A. The fields started to smell.

   B. The gardens produced more flowers.

   C. The land was ruined.

   D. The rivers became too deep.

4. How did President Ot feel about the plan and attempt to trick Earth?

   A. He felt ashamed.

   B. He felt proud.

   C. He felt confused.

   D. He felt worried.

5. Why can't the Tyrrans get food and water from Earth?

   A. The Lambchops don't want to help the Tyrrans.

   B. The Tyrrans don't know how to get to Earth.

   C. There is not enough food and water on Earth to give to the Tyrrans.

   D. There is no easy way to get food and water from Earth to Tyrra.

Check Your Reading Speed

1분에 몇 단어를 읽는지 리딩 속도를 측정해보세요.

$$\frac{763 \ words}{reading \ time \ (\qquad) \ sec} \times 60 = (\qquad) \ WPM$$

Build Your Vocabulary

☀ **nod** [nad] v. (고개를) 끄덕이다, 까딱하다; n. (고개를) 끄덕임
If you nod in a particular direction, you bend your head once in that direction in order to indicate something or to give someone a signal.

go on idiom 자자, 어서; (어떤 상황이) 계속되다; 말을 계속하다
'Go on' is used to encourage or dare someone to do something.

복습 **dear** [diər] n. 여보, 당신; 얘야; int. 이런!, 맙소사!; a. 사랑하는; ~에게
You can call someone dear as a sign of affection.

☀ **drum** [drʌm] v. 계속 두드리다; 북을 치다; n. 북, 드럼
If something drums on a surface, or if you drum something on a surface, it hits it regularly, making a continuous beating sound.

복습 **faint** [feint] a. 희미한, 약한; v. 실신하다, 기절하다; n. 실신, 기절 (faintly ad. 희미하게)
A faint sound, color, mark, feeling, or quality has very little strength or intensity.

복습 **scout** [skaut] n. 정찰병; 스카우트; v. (무엇을 찾아) 돌아다니다; 정찰하다
A scout is someone who is sent to an area of countryside to find out the position of an enemy army.

☀ **cozy** [kóuzi] a. 아늑한, 편안한; 친밀한
A house or room that is cozy is comfortable and warm.

‡ **scene** [siːn] n. 장면, 광경; 현장; 풍경
You refer to a place as a scene when you are describing its appearance and indicating what impression it makes on you.

‡ **occupy** [ákjupài] v. 사용하다; (공간·지역·시간을) 차지하다; 바쁘게 하다
If a room or something such as a seat is occupied, someone is using it, so that it is not available for anyone else.

atop [ətáp] prep. 꼭대기에, 맨 위에
If something is atop something else, it is on top of it.

thumbtack [θʌ́mtæk] n. 압정; v. 압정으로 고정시키다
A thumbtack is a short pin with a broad flat top which is used for fastening papers or pictures to a board, wall, or other surface.

복습 **serve** [səːrv] v. (특정한 용도로) 쓰일 수 있다; (조직·국가 등을 위해) 일하다; (상품·서비스를) 제공하다
If something serves as a particular thing or serves a particular purpose, it performs a particular function, which is often not its intended function.

‡ **stool** [stuːl] n. (등받이와 팔걸이가 없는) 의자, 스툴
A stool is a seat with legs but no support for your arms or back.

‡ **sip** [sip] v. (음료를) 홀짝거리다, 조금씩 마시다; n. 한 모금
If you sip a drink or sip at it, you drink by taking just a small amount at a time.

‡ **fashion** [fǽʃən] v. (손으로) 만들다; n. 유행; 패션
If you fashion an object or a work of art, you make it.

‡ **nibble** [nibl] v. 조금씩 먹다; 약간 관심을 보이다; n. 한 입
If you nibble food, you eat it by biting very small pieces of it, for example because you are not very hungry.

crumb [krʌm] n. (빵·케이크의) 부스러기; 약간, 소량
Crumbs are tiny pieces that fall from bread, biscuits, or cake when you cut it or eat it.

^{복습}**sigh** [sai] v. 한숨을 쉬다, 한숨짓다; 탄식하듯 말하다; n. 한숨
When you sigh, you let out a deep breath, as a way of expressing feelings such as disappointment, tiredness, or pleasure.

^{복습}**observe** [əbzə́ːrv] v. ~을 보다; 관찰하다; (발언·의견을) 말하다
If you observe someone or something, you see or notice them.

^{복습}**refresh** [rifréʃ] v. 생기를 되찾게 하다; ~의 기억을 새롭게 하다
(refreshment n. (pl.) 다과)
Refreshments are drinks and small amounts of food that are provided, for example, during a meeting or a journey.

^{복습}**fit** [fit] a. 적합한, 알맞은; 건강한; v. (모양·크기가) 맞다; 적절하다
If something is fit for a particular purpose, it is suitable for that purpose.

[★]**tin** [tin] n. 통조림
A tin is a metal container which is filled with food and sealed in order to preserve the food for long periods of time.

have in store idiom 준비해 두다
If you have something in store, you have it prepared.

make a face idiom 얼굴을 찌푸리다, 침울한 표정을 짓다
If you make a face, you twist your face to indicate a certain mental or emotional state.

^{복습}**spread** [spred] n. 스프레드(빵에 발라 먹는 식품); 확산, 전파; v. 펼치다; 퍼뜨리다, 확산시키다
Spread is a soft food which is put on bread.

spinach [spíniʧ] n. 시금치
Spinach is a vegetable with large dark green leaves that you chop up and boil in water before eating.

[★]**dreadful** [drédfəl] a. 끔찍한, 지독한; 무시무시한
If you say that something is dreadful, you mean that it is very bad or unpleasant, or very poor in quality.

never mind idiom 신경 쓰지 마

You use never mind to tell someone that they need not do something or worry about something, because it is not important or because you will do it yourself.

tragedy [trǽdʒədi] n. 비극

A tragedy is an extremely sad event or situation.

invent [invént] v. 발명하다; (사실이 아닌 것을) 지어내다 (invention n. 발명품)

An invention is a machine, device, or system that has been invented by someone.

double [dʌbl] v. 두 배로 만들다; a. 두 배의, 갑절의; 이중의; n. 두 배, 갑절

When something doubles or when you double it, it becomes twice as great in number, amount, or size.

crop [krap] n. 수확량; (농)작물

The plants or fruits that are collected at harvest time are referred to as a crop.

brew [bruː] v. 양조하다; (커피·차를) 끓이다; n. 혼합

If a person or company brews beer, they make it.

smelly [sméli] a. 냄새 나는

Something that is smelly has an unpleasant smell.

vat [væt] n. 큰 통, 큰 탱크; v. 큰 통에 넣다

A vat is a large barrel or tank in which liquids can be stored.

planet [plǽnit] n. [천문] 행성

A planet is a large, round object in space that moves around a star.

stroll [stroul] v. 거닐다, 산책하다; n. (한가로이) 거닐기, 산책

If you stroll somewhere, you walk there in a slow, relaxed way.

mishap [míshæp] n. 작은 사고

A mishap is an unfortunate but not very serious event that happens to someone.

★ murmur [mə́:rmər] v. 속삭이다, 소곤거리다, 중얼거리다; n. 속삭임, 소곤거림
If you murmur something, you say it very quietly, so that not many people can hear what you are saying.

복습 bark [ba:rk] v. (명령·질문 등을) 빽 내지르다; (개가) 짖다; n. 나무껍질; (개 등이) 짖는 소리
If you bark at someone, you shout at them aggressively in a loud, rough voice.

★ stuff [stʌf] n. 것, 물건; v. 채워 넣다; 쑤셔 넣다
You can use stuff to refer to things such as a substance, a collection of things, events, or ideas, or the contents of something in a general way without mentioning the thing itself by name.

★ explode [iksplóud] v. 폭발하다; 폭발적으로 증가하다; 갑자기 ~하다
If an object such as a bomb explodes or if someone or something explodes it, it bursts loudly and with great force, often causing damage or injury.

hang one's head idiom 부끄러워 고개를 떨구다
If you hang your head, you look downward because you feel ashamed.

★ boom [bu:m] n. 쾅 (하는 소리); v. 굵은 목소리로 말하다; 쾅 하는 소리를 내다
Boom is a deep loud sound that continues for some time, for example the noise of thunder or an explosion.

★ shatter [ʃǽtər] v. 산산이 부수다, 산산조각 내다; 엄청난 충격을 주다
If something shatters or is shattered, it breaks into a lot of small pieces.

복습 roof [ru:f] n. 지붕; v. 지붕을 씌우다
The roof of a building is the covering on top of it that protects the people and things inside from the weather.

thank goodness idiom 정말 다행이다!
You say 'thank God' or 'thank goodness' when you are very relieved about something.

복습 darken [dá:rkən] v. 어두워지다; 우울해지다
If something darkens or if a person or thing darkens it, it becomes darker.

tremendous [triméndəs] a. 엄청난; 굉장한, 대단한
You use tremendous to emphasize how strong a feeling or quality is, or how large an amount is.

field [fiːld] n. 들판, 밭; ~장; 분야; 현장
A field is an area of grass, for example in a park or on a farm.

greenery [gríːnəri] n. 녹색 나무
Plants that make a place look attractive are referred to as greenery.

★**pace** [peis] v. 서성거리다; (일의) 속도를 유지하다; n. 속도; 걸음
If you pace a small area, you keep walking up and down it, because you are anxious or impatient.

back and forth idiom 앞뒤로; 좌우로; 여기저기에, 왔다갔다
If someone moves back and forth, they repeatedly move in one direction and then in the opposite direction.

★**prove** [pruːv] v. 입증하다, 증명하다; (~임이) 드러나다
If you prove that something is true, you show by means of argument or evidence that it is definitely true.

broadcast [brɔ́ːdkæst] v. (broadcast-broadcast) 널리 알리다, 광고하다; 방송하다; n. 방송
To broadcast means to tell people something, especially something that you wanted to be a secret.

at once idiom 즉시; 동시에
If you do something at once, you do it immediately.

★**despair** [dispέər] v. 절망하다, 체념하다; n. 절망
If you despair, you feel that everything is wrong and that nothing will improve.

recover [rikʌ́vər] v. 회복되다; (의식 등을) 되찾다; (손실 등을) 되찾다
If something recovers from a period of weakness or difficulty, it improves or gets stronger again.

* **panic** [pǽnik] n. 극심한 공포, 공황; v. 겁에 질려 어쩔 줄 모르다, 공황 상태에 빠지다
Panic or a panic is a situation in which people are affected by a strong feeling of anxiety.

* **lure** [luər] v. 꾀다, 유혹하다; n. 유혹, 매력
To lure someone means to trick them into a particular place or to trick them into doing something that they should not do.

복습 **spaceship** [spéisʃip] n. 우주선
A spaceship is a rocket or other vehicle that carries people through space.

ransom [rǽnsəm] n. (납치·유괴된 사람에 대한) 몸값; v. 몸값을 지불하다
(hold for ransom idiom ~을 억류하고 몸값을 요구하다)
If someone is holding you for ransom, they are using their power to try to force you to do something which you do not want to do.

* **shameful** [ʃéimfəl] a. 수치스러운, 창피한, 부끄러운
If you describe a person's action or attitude as shameful, you think that it is so bad that the person ought to be ashamed.

underhand [ʌndərhǽnd] a. (= underhanded) 비밀의, 부정직한
If an action is underhand or if it is done in an underhand way, it is done secretly and dishonestly.

복습 **trail away** idiom (목소리가) 차츰 잦아들다
If a speaker's voice or a speaker trails away, their voice becomes quieter and they hesitate until they stop speaking completely.

patter [pǽtər] n. 후두두 하는 소리; v. 후두두 하는 소리를 내다
A patter is a series of quick, quiet, tapping sounds.

복습 **particular** [pərtíkjulər] a. 특별한; 특정한; 까다로운; n. 자세한 사실
(particularly ad. 특히, 특별히)
Particularly means more than usual or more than other things.

* **conquer** [káŋkər] v. (다른 나라나 민족을) 정복하다; 이기다; 극복하다
If one country or group of people conquers another, they take complete control of their land.

willing [wíliŋ] a. 기꺼이 하는, 자발적인; ~에 반대하지 않는
(willingly ad. 자진해서, 기꺼이)
If someone is willing to do something, they are fairly happy about doing it and will do it if they are asked or required to do it.

bless [bles] v. (신의) 축복을 빌다 (bless you idiom 축복이 있기를)
Bless is used in expressions such as 'God bless' or 'bless you' to express affection, thanks, or good wishes.

clap [klæp] v. 박수를 치다; (갑자기·재빨리) 놓다; n. 박수; 쿵 하는 소리
When you clap, you hit your hands together to show appreciation or attract attention.

gasp [gæsp] v. 숨이 턱 막히다, 헉 하고 숨을 쉬다; n. 헉 하는 소리를 냄
When you gasp, you take a short quick breath through your mouth, especially when you are surprised, shocked, or in pain.

hardly [háːrdli] ad. 거의 ~할 수가 없다; 거의 ~아니다; ~하자마자
When you say you can hardly do something, you are emphasizing that it is very difficult for you to do it.

terrible [térəbl] a. 끔찍한, 소름끼치는; 형편없는; (나쁜 정도가) 극심한
A terrible experience or situation is very serious or very unpleasant.

cupboard [kʌ́bərd] n. 찬장; 벽장
A cupboard is a piece of furniture that has one or two doors, usually contains shelves, and is used to store things.

starve [staːrv] v. 굶주리다, 굶어죽다
If people starve, they suffer greatly from lack of food which sometimes leads to their death.

Stanley's Good Idea

1. What was the atmosphere like on the *Star Scout* at first?

   A. It was unusual.

   B. It was unhappy.

   C. It was hopeful.

   D. It was cheerful.

2. What did the Tyrrans think of the population of Earth?

   A. They thought it was strange that the population was so small.

   B. They thought it was unimpressive that the population was big.

   C. They thought it was unbelievable that so many people lived on Earth.

   D. They thought it was funny that Earth didn't have a lot of people.

3. What did the Lambchops think of the population of Tyrra?

A. They were surprised that there weren't that many Tyrrans.

B. They were impressed that the population was huge.

C. They were worried that there were too many Tyrrans.

D. They were disappointed that Tyrra didn't have a large population.

4. Why did Stanley ask Mrs. Ot how much she weighed?

A. He wanted to compare his weight with Mrs. Ot's.

B. He wanted to know the average weight of a Tyrran.

C. He wanted to find out how healthy Mrs. Ot was.

D. He wanted to check if Mrs. Ot had lost any weight.

5. Why did Mr. Lambchop tell the General to bring all Tyrrans to the Star Scout?

A. Mr. Lambchop was hoping everyone could live together on the spaceship.

B. Mr. Lambchop was planning to count the number of Tyrrans on the planet.

C. Mr. Lambchop thought everyone could travel together to Earth.

D. Mr. Lambchop wanted to eat tinned food and drink Grape Fizzola with the Tyrrans.

Check Your Reading Speed
1분에 몇 단어를 읽는지 리딩 속도를 측정해보세요.

$$\frac{392 \text{ words}}{\text{reading time ( ) sec}} \times 60 = (\quad) \text{ WPM}$$

Build Your Vocabulary

✴ **pot** [pat] n. 그릇; 냄비; 항아리; v. (나무를) 화분에 심다 (teapot n. 찻주전자)
A teapot is a container with a lid, a handle, and a spout, used for making and serving tea.

복습 **crumb** [krʌm] n. (빵·케이크의) 부스러기; 약간, 소량
Crumbs are tiny pieces that fall from bread, biscuits, or cake when you cut it or eat it.

✴ **plate** [pleit] n. 접시, 그릇; 판; (자동차) 번호판
A plate is a round or oval flat dish that is used to hold food.

✴ **gloom** [gluːm] n. 우울, 침울; 어둠
Gloom is a feeling of sadness and lack of hope.

복습 **cheerful** [ʧíərfəl] a. 발랄한, 쾌활한; 쾌적한
Someone who is cheerful is happy and shows this in their behavior.

복습 **tin** [tin] n. 통조림 (tinned a. 통조림으로 된)
Tinned food is food that has been preserved by being sealed in a tin.

✴✴ **plenty** [plénti] n. 풍부한 양; 풍요로움; ad. 많이
If there are plenty of things, there are many of them.

✴ **thankful** [θǽŋkfəl] a. 고맙게 생각하는, 감사하는
When you are thankful, you are very happy and relieved that something has happened.

amaze [əméiz] v. (대단히) 놀라게 하다; 경악하게 하다 (amazed a. (대단히) 놀란)
If something amazes you, it surprises you very much.

joke [dʒouk] v. 농담하다; 농담 삼아 말하다; n. 농담; 웃음거리
You say 'you're joking' to someone when they have just told you something that is so surprising or unreasonable that you find it difficult to believe.

president [prézədənt] n. 대통령; 회장
The president of a country that has no king or queen is the person who is the head of state of that country.

dreadful [drédfəl] a. 끔찍한, 지독한; 무시무시한
Dreadful is used to emphasize the degree or extent of something bad.

crush [krʌʃ] n. (좁은 곳에) 잔뜩 몰려든 군중; v. (자신감이나 행복을) 짓밟다; 으스러뜨리다
A crush is a crowd of people close together, in which it is difficult to move.

youthful [júːθfəl] a. 젊은이 특유의, 젊은이다운
Someone who is youthful behaves as if they are young or younger than they really are.

marriage [mǽridʒ] n. 결혼 (생활)
A marriage is the relationship between a husband and wife.

population [pàpjuléiʃən] n. 인구, (모든) 주민
The population of a country or area is all the people who live in it.

capital [kǽpətl] n. 수도; 자본금, 자금; 자산; a. 대문자의
The capital of a country is the city or town where its government or parliament meets.

gosh [gaʃ] int. (놀람·기쁨을 나타내어) 어머!, 뭐라고!
Some people say 'Gosh' when they are surprised.

bet [bet] v. ~이 틀림없다; (내기 등에) 돈을 걸다; n. 내기; 짐작, 추측
You use expressions such as 'I bet,' 'I'll bet,' and 'you can bet' to indicate that you are sure something is true.

‡ **weigh** [wei] v. 무게가 ~이다; 무게를 달다
If someone or something weighs a particular amount, this amount is how heavy they are.

＊**offend** [əfénd] v. 기분 상하게 하다; 불쾌하게 여겨지다; 범죄를 저지르다
If you offend someone, you say or do something rude which upsets or embarrasses them.

＊**slim** [slim] v. 날씬해지려 하다; a. 날씬한, 호리호리한
If you are slimming, you are trying to make yourself thinner and lighter by eating less food.

＊**hip** [hip] n. 엉덩이
Your hips are the two areas at the sides of your body between the tops of your legs and your waist.

‡ **rush** [rʌʃ] v. 급히 움직이다; 서두르다; 재촉하다; n. 혼잡, 분주함; a. 급한; 바쁜
If you rush something, you do it in a hurry, often too quickly and without much care.

‡ **average** [ǽvəridʒ] a. 보통의, 일반적인; 평균의; n. 평균
An average person or thing is typical or normal.

put together idiom ~을 합치다, 합계하다
To put together means to group together some set of people or things.

figure out idiom 계산하다, 산출하다; ~을 이해하다, 알아내다
If you figure something out, you calculate the total amount of it.

＊**lad** [læd] n. 사내애; 청년
A lad is a young man or boy.

＊**summon** [sʌ́mən] v. 호출하다, (오라고) 부르다; 소환하다
If you summon someone, you order them to come to you.

복습 **fetch** [fetʃ] v. 가지고 오다, 데리고 오다; (특정 가격에) 팔리다; n. 가져옴, 데려옴
If you fetch something or someone, you go and get them from the place where they are.

remain [riméin] n. (pl.) 남은 것, 나머지; v. 계속 ~이다; 남다

The remains of something are the parts of it that are left after most of it has been taken away or destroyed.

The Weighing

1. What did the *Star Scout* booklet say?

   A. Friends should not be brought aboard the spacecraft.

   B. Only small souvenirs can be stored in the spacecraft.

   C. The spacecraft is not meant to be comfortable.

   D. The spacecraft is only safe for humans.

2. How were the Tyrrans weighed?

   A. All of the Tyrrans were weighed at the same time.

   B. Each Tyrran family was weighed separately.

   C. The Tyrrans were weighed one at a time.

   D. The Tyrrans were weighed in groups.

3. **What happened right after the Tyrrans and their supplies were weighed?**

A. All of the Tyrrans got on the *Star Scout*.

B. The tinned food and Fizzola were thrown away.

C. The Lambchops got rid of some of their stuff.

D. President Ot gave a speech.

4. **What was NOT mentioned as something the Lambchops discarded?**

A. Extra clothes

B. Music posters

C. A bed

D. A board game

5. **Why did President Ot volunteer to stay behind?**

A. He was too nervous to go to Earth.

B. He needed to look after the planet while everyone was gone.

C. He didn't want to travel without Mrs. Ot.

D. He wanted to reduce the total weight of the nation.

Check Your Reading Speed
1분에 몇 단어를 읽는지 리딩 속도를 측정해보세요.

$$\frac{715 \text{ words}}{\text{reading time ( ) sec}} \times 60 = (\quad) \text{ WPM}$$

Build Your Vocabulary

복습 **weigh** [wei] v. 무게가 ~이다; 무게를 달다 (weighing n. 계량)
If someone or something weighs a particular amount, this amount is how heavy they are.

☆ **guard** [gɑːrd] n. 경비 요원; 감시, 경호; v. 지키다, 보호하다; 감시하다
A guard is someone such as a soldier, police officer, or prison officer who is guarding a particular place or person.

복습 **jail** [dʒeil] n. 교도소, 감옥; v. 수감하다
A jail is a place where criminals are kept in order to punish them, or where people waiting to be tried are kept.

복습 **field** [fiːld] n. 들판, 밭; ~장; 분야; 현장
A field is an area of grass, for example in a park or on a farm.

복습 **tiny** [táini] a. 아주 작은
Something or someone that is tiny is extremely small.

★ **assemble** [əsémbl] v. 모이다, 집합시키다; 조립하다
When people assemble or when someone assembles them, they come together in a group, usually for a particular purpose such as a meeting.

복습 **address** [ədrés] v. 연설하다; 말을 걸다; 주소를 쓰다; n. 주소; 연설
If you address a group of people, you give a speech to them.

90

복습 fellow [félou] a. 동료의; n. 녀석, 친구; 동료
You use fellow to describe people who are in the same situation as you, or people you feel you have something in common with.

confess [kənfés] v. 고백하다, 인정하다; 자백하다
If someone confesses to doing something wrong, they admit that they did it.

deceive [disíːv] v. 속이다, 기만하다
If you deceive someone, you make them believe something that is not true, usually in order to get some advantage for yourself.

stream [striːm] n. 개울, 시내; (액체·기체의) 줄기; v. (액체·기체가) 줄줄 흐르다
A stream is a small narrow river.

복습 fit [fit] a. 적합한, 알맞은; 건강한; v. (모양·크기가) 맞다; 적절하다
If something is fit for a particular purpose, it is suitable for that purpose.

복습 crowd [kraud] n. 사람들, 군중; v. 가득 메우다; (생각이 마음속에) 밀려오다
A crowd is a large group of people who have gathered together.

lordy [lɔ́ːrdi] int. 저런, 어머
You can say 'lordy' as an exclamation of surprise or dismay.

talk about idiom (강조의 뜻으로) ~하기란
You can say talk about before mentioning a particular expression or situation, when you mean that something is a very striking or clear example of that expression or situation.

복습 starve [staːrv] v. 굶주리다, 굶어죽다
If people starve, they suffer greatly from lack of food which sometimes leads to their death.

refuge [réfjuːdʒ] n. 피난(처), 도피처; 보호 시설, 쉼터
If you take refuge somewhere, you try to protect yourself from physical harm by going there.

복습 voyage [vɔ́iidʒ] n. 여행, 항해; v. 여행하다, 항해하다
A voyage is a long journey on a ship or in a spacecraft.

attention [əténʃən] n. 주의 (집중), 주목; 관심, 흥미
(pay attention idiom 주의를 기울이다)
If you pay attention to someone, you watch them, listen to them, or take notice of them.

booklet [búklit] n. 작은 책자, 팸플릿
A booklet is a small book that has a paper cover and that gives you information about something.

scout [skaut] n. 정찰병; 스카우트; v. (무엇을 찾아) 돌아다니다; 정찰하다
A scout is someone who is sent to an area of countryside to find out the position of an enemy army.

design [dizáin] v. 고안하다; 설계하다; 만들다; n. 디자인; 설계도, 도안
If something is designed for a particular purpose, it is intended for that purpose.

comfort [kʌ́mfərt] n. 안락, 편안; 위로, 위안; v. 위로하다, 위안하다
If you are doing something in comfort, you are physically relaxed and contented, and are not feeling any pain or other unpleasant sensations.

weight [weit] n. 무게, 체중; 무거운 것
The weight of a person or thing is how heavy they are, measured in units such as kilograms, pounds, or tons.

souvenir [sùːvəníər] n. 기념품
A souvenir is something which you buy or keep to remind you of a holiday, place, or event.

aboard [əbɔ́ːrd] ad. (배·기차·비행기 등에) 탄, 탑승한
If you are aboard a ship or plane, you are on it or in it.

have had it idiom 끝장나다; 완전히 지치다
If you say that someone has had it, you mean they are in very serious trouble or have no hope of succeeding.

supply [səplái] n. (pl.) 용품, 비품; 비축(량); 공급; v. 공급하다, 제공하다
You can use supplies to refer to food, equipment, and other essential things that people need, especially when these are provided in large quantities.

require [rikwáiər] v. 필요로 하다, 요구하다
If you require something or if something is required, you need it or it is necessary.

scale [skeil] n. 저울; 규모, 범위; 눈금; v. 오르다
Scales are a piece of equipment used for weighing things.

prove [pru:v] v. (~임이) 드러나다; 입증하다, 증명하다
If something proves to be true or to have a particular quality, it becomes clear after a period of time that it is true or has that quality.

brief [bri:f] a. (시간이) 짧은; 간단한; v. ~에게 보고하다 (briefly ad. 잠시)
Something that happens or is done briefly happens or is done for a very short period of time.

delay [diléi] v. 지연시키다; 미루다, 연기하다; n. 지연, 지체
To delay someone or something means to make them late or to slow them down.

board [bɔːrd] n. 판; 이사회; v. 승선하다, 탑승하다
A board is a square piece of wood or stiff cardboard that you use for playing games such as chess.

ramp [ræmp] n. 경사로, 진입로; (항공기의) 이동식 계단
A ramp is a sloping surface between two places that are at different levels.

mount [maunt] v. 올라가다; 시작하다; 증가하다; n. 산
If you mount the stairs or a platform, you go up the stairs or go up onto the platform.

bark [ba:rk] v. (명령·질문 등을) 빽 내지르다; (개가) 짖다; n. 나무껍질; (개 등이) 짖는 소리
If you bark at someone, you shout at them aggressively in a loud, rough voice.

jiggle [dʒigl] v. (빠르게) 움직이다; 까불다
To jiggle around means to move quickly up and down or from side to side.

march [maːrʧ] v. 행진하다; (단호한 태도로 급히) 걸어가다; n. 행군, 행진; 3월
When soldiers march somewhere, or when a commanding officer marches them somewhere, they walk there with very regular steps, as a group.

pad [pæd] n. 메모장; (우주선 등의) 발사대; v. ~에 덧대다
A pad of paper is a number of pieces of paper which are fixed together along the top or the side, so that each piece can be torn off when it has been used.

take care idiom ~을 처리하다; ~을 돌보다
If you take care to do something, you make sure that you do it.

needle [niːdl] n. (계기의) 바늘, 지침; (주사) 바늘, 침
On an instrument which measures something such as speed or weight, the needle is the long strip of metal or plastic on the dial that moves backward and forward, showing the measurement.

still [stil] a. 가만히 있는, 정지한; ad. 아직(도) (계속해서)
If you stay still, you stay in the same position and do not move.

entire [intáiər] a. 전체의, 온
You use entire when you want to emphasize that you are referring to the whole of something.

population [pàpjuléiʃən] n. 인구, (모든) 주민
The population of a country or area is all the people who live in it.

tin [tin] n. 통조림 (tinned a. 통조림으로 된)
Tinned food is food that has been preserved by being sealed in a tin.

announce [ənáuns] v. 발표하다, 알리다; 선언하다
If you announce something, you tell people about it publicly or officially.

lighten [laitn] v. 가볍게 하다; (일·부채·걱정 등을) 덜어 주다; 밝게 하다
If you lighten something, you make it less heavy.

discard [diskáːrd] v. 버리다, 폐기하다
If you discard something, you get rid of it because you no longer want it or need it.

bunk [bʌŋk] n. (배나 기차의) 침상; 이층 침대; v. 침대에서 자다
A bunk is a bed that is fixed to a wall, especially in a ship or trailer.

chief [ʧiːf] a. (계급·직급상) 최고위자인; n. (조직·집단의) 장(長)
Chief is used in the job titles of the most senior worker or workers of a particular kind in an organization.

pilot [páilət] n. 조종사, 비행사
A pilot is a person who is trained to fly an aircraft.

zip [zip] n. 지퍼; v. 지퍼를 잠그다; (어떤 방향으로) 쌩 하고 가다
A zip or zip fastener is a device used to open and close parts of clothes and bags.

flag [flæg] n. 기, 깃발; v. 표시를 하다; 지치다; 약해지다
A flag is a piece of cloth which can be attached to a pole and which is used as a sign, signal, or symbol of something, especially of a particular country.

knee [niː] n. 무릎; v. 무릎으로 치다
Your knee is the place where your leg bends.

gorilla [gərílə] n. [동물] 고릴라
A gorilla is a very large ape. It has long arms, black fur, and a black face.

smuggle [smʌgl] v. 밀반입하다, 밀수하다
If someone smuggles things or people into a place or out of it, they take them there illegally or secretly.

kitchenware [kíʧənwɛər] n. 주방용품
Kitchenware is things that are used for preparing and eating food, for example knives, dishes, and pans.

hush [hʌʃ] v. ~을 조용히 시키다; 진정시키다, 달래다; n. 침묵, 고요 (hushed a. 조용한)
A hushed place is peaceful and much quieter and calmer than usual.

pile [pail] n. 쌓아 놓은 것, 더미; 무더기; v. (차곡차곡) 쌓다; 우르르 가다
A pile of things is a mass of them that is high in the middle and has sloping sides.

scold [skould] v. 야단치다, 꾸짖다
If you scold someone, you speak angrily to them because they have done something wrong.

dear [diər] int. 이런!, 맙소사!; n. 여보, 당신; 얘야; a. ~에게
You can use dear in expressions such as 'oh dear,' 'dear me,' and 'dear, dear' when you are sad, disappointed, or surprised about something.

whisper [hwíspər] v. 속삭이다, 소곤거리다; n. 속삭임, 소곤거리는 소리
When you whisper, you say something very quietly, using your breath rather than your throat, so that only one person can hear you.

cheer [ʧiər] n. 환호(성), 응원의 함성; v. 기운이 나다; 환호성을 지르다, 환호하다
A cheer is a loud shout of happiness or approval.

volunteer [vàləntíər] n. 자원하는 사람; 자원 봉사자; v. 자원하다; 제안하다
A volunteer is someone who offers to do a particular task or job without being forced to do it.

murmur [mə́:rmər] n. 속삭임, 소곤거림; v. 속삭이다, 소곤거리다, 중얼거리다
A murmur is something that is said which can hardly be heard.

resolve [rizálv] v. (문제 등을) 해결하다; 결심하다, 결의하다; n. 결심
To resolve a problem, argument, or difficulty means to find a solution to it.

regain [rigéin] v. 되찾다, 회복하다; 되돌아오다
If you regain something that you have lost, you get it back again.

popularity [pàpjulǽrəti] n. 인기
Popularity is the fact that something or someone is liked, enjoyed, or supported by many people.

★ **fade** [feid] v. 서서히 사라지다, 점점 희미해지다; 바래다, 희미해지다
If memories, feelings, or possibilities fade, they slowly become less intense or less strong.

Heading Home

1. Where did the Tyrrans sit in the *Star Scout?*

A. They sat in the corner of the spacecraft.

B. They sat inside the refrigerator.

C. They sat in many different places.

D. They sat in the Chief Pilot's seat.

2. What had Mrs. Lambchop done for the Tyrrans?

A. She had written a song for them.

B. She had created blankets and pillows for them.

C. She had cleared space on the shelves for them.

D. She had prepared food for them.

3. What did Captain Ik do before takeoff?

    A. He made Arthur put him on another shelf.

    B. He asked Mrs. Lambchop for advice on living on Earth.

    C. He thanked Arthur for being so kind to him.

    D. He apologized to Mrs. Lambchop for trying to harm Arthur.

4. What did the Lambchops think of the Tyrran national anthem?

    A. They thought the national anthem was creative.

    B. They thought the national anthem was a little silly.

    C. They thought the national anthem was touching.

    D. They thought the national anthem was very similar to theirs.

5. Why was Stanley satisfied with the journey to Tyrra?

    A. He felt that the Lambchops had fulfilled their mission.

    B. He figured that he had seen enough of the planet.

    C. He believed that the Lambchops had tried their best to be nice to everyone.

    D. He thought that he had done a good job steering the *Star Scout*.

Check Your Reading Speed

1분에 몇 단어를 읽는지 리딩 속도를 측정해보세요.

$$\frac{398 \text{ words}}{\text{reading time ( ) sec}} \times 60 = (\quad) \text{ WPM}$$

Build Your Vocabulary

복습 **president** [prézədənt] n. 대통령; 회장
The president of a country that has no king or queen is the person who is the head of state of that country.

* **ledge** [ledʒ] n. (벽에서 튀어나온) 선반; 절벽에서 튀어나온 바위
A ledge is a narrow shelf along the bottom edge of a window.

복습 **magnify** [mǽgnəfài] v. 확대하다; 과장하다
To magnify an object means to make it appear larger than it really is, by means of a special lens or mirror.

* **fridge** [fridʒ] n. (= refrigerator) 냉장고
A fridge is a large metal container which is kept cool, usually by electricity, so that food that is put in it stays fresh.

nook [nuk] n. (아늑하고 조용한) 곳
A nook is a small and sheltered place.

cranny [krǽni] n. (pl.) (작은) 구멍
Crannies are very narrow openings or spaces in something.

복습 **cupboard** [kʌ́bərd] n. 찬장; 벽장
A cupboard is a piece of furniture that has one or two doors, usually contains shelves, and is used to store things.

sheet [ʃiːt] n. (침대) 시트; (종이) 한 장
A sheet is a large rectangular piece of cotton or other cloth that you sleep on or cover yourself with in a bed.

blanket [blǽŋkit] n. 담요, 모포; v. (완전히) 뒤덮다
A blanket is a large square or rectangular piece of thick cloth, especially one which you put on a bed to keep you warm.

pillow [pílou] n. 베개
A pillow is a rectangular cushion which you rest your head on when you are in bed.

makeshift [méikʃift] a. 임시변통의
Makeshift things are temporary and usually of poor quality, but they are used because there is nothing better available.

settle [setl] v. 자리를 잡다; (떨어져·내려) 앉다; 해결하다
If you settle yourself somewhere or settle somewhere, you sit down or make yourself comfortable.

notice [nóutis] n. 알림, 통지, 예고; 주목, 알아챔; v. 의식하다; 주목하다
If you give notice about something that is going to happen, you give a warning in advance that it is going to happen.

edge [edʒ] n. 끝, 가장자리, 모서리; 위기; v. 조금씩 움직이다
The edge of something is the place or line where it stops, or the part of it that is furthest from the middle.

chief [ʧiːf] a. (계급·직급상) 최고위자인; n. (조직·집단의) 장(長)
Chief is used in the job titles of the most senior worker or workers of a particular kind in an organization.

pilot [páilət] n. 조종사, 비행사
A pilot is a person who is trained to fly an aircraft.

shelf [ʃelf] n. 선반; (책장의) 칸
A shelf is a flat piece of wood, metal, or glass which is attached to a wall or to the sides of a cupboard.

^{복습} **whisper** [hwíspər] v. 속삭이다, 소곤거리다; n. 속삭임, 소곤거리는 소리
When you whisper, you say something very quietly, using your breath rather than your throat, so that only one person can hear you.

[*] **apologize** [əpálədʒàiz] v. 사과하다 (apology n. 사과)
An apology is something that you say or write in order to tell someone that you are sorry that you have hurt them or caused trouble for them.

^{복습} **attempt** [ətémpt] v. 시도하다, 애써 해보다; n. 시도
If you attempt to do something, especially something difficult, you try to do it.

^{복습} **paralyze** [pǽrəlàiz] v. 마비시키다; 무력하게 하다; 쓸모없게 하다
If someone is paralyzed by an accident or an illness, they have no feeling in their body, or in part of their body, and are unable to move.

^{복습} **dear** [diər] n. 얘야; 여보, 당신; int. 이런!, 맙소사!; a. ~에게
You can call someone dear as a sign of affection.

^{복습} **attention** [əténʃən] n. 주의 (집중), 주목; 관심, 흥미
If someone or something attracts your attention or catches your attention, you suddenly notice them.

anthem [ǽnθəm] n. (국가·단체 등의) 노래; 성가
An anthem is a song which is used to represent a particular nation, society, or group and which is sung on special occasions.

[*] **hum** [hʌm] v. 콧노래를 부르다, (노래를) 흥얼거리다; 윙윙거리다; n. 윙윙거리는 소리
When you hum a tune, you sing it with your lips closed.

[*] **key** [kiː] n. 가락, 조; 열쇠, 키; a. 핵심적인, 필수적인
In music, a key is a scale of musical notes that starts on one specific note.

^{복습} **planet** [plǽnit] n. [천문] 행성
A planet is a large, round object in space that moves around a star.

[*] **roam** [roum] v. (이리저리) 돌아다니다; (시선·손이) 천천히 훑다
If you roam an area or roam around it, you wander or travel around it without having a particular purpose.

* **echo** [ékou] v. (소리가) 울리다, 메아리치다; 그대로 따라 하다; n. (소리의) 울림, 메아리
If a sound echoes, it is reflected off a surface and can be heard again after the original sound has stopped.

* **cabin** [kǽbin] n. (항공기·배의) 선실; (나무로 된) 오두막집
A cabin is one of the areas inside a plane.

* **weep** [wi:p] v. 울다, 눈물을 흘리다; 물기를 내뿜다; n. 울기
If someone weeps, they cry.

glisten [glisn] v. 반짝이다, 번들거리다
If something glistens, it shines, usually because it is wet or oily.

* **humble** [hʌmbl] a. 보잘것없는; 겸손한; 변변치 않은; v. 겸손하게 만들다; 쉽게 이기다
A humble place or thing is ordinary and not special in any way.

복습 **press** [pres] v. 누르다; (무엇에) 바짝 대다; 밀다; n. 언론; 인쇄
If you press a button or switch, you push it with your finger in order to make a machine or device work.

복습 **roar** [rɔ:r] v. (크고 깊은 소리로) 울리다; 고함치다; n. 함성; 울부짖는 듯한 소리
If something roars, it makes a very loud noise.

복습 **gain** [gein] v. 쌓다, 늘리다; (이익·혜택을) 얻다; n. 증가; 이득
To gain something such as weight or speed means to have an increase in that particular thing.

복습 **mission** [míʃən] n. 임무; 우주 비행
A mission is an important task that people are given to do, especially one that involves traveling to another country.

* **distant** [dístənt] a. 먼, (멀리) 떨어져 있는; 다정하지 않은
Distant means very far away.

복습 **satisfy** [sǽtisfài] v. 만족시키다; 충족시키다 (satisfactory a. 만족스러운, 충분한)
Something that is satisfactory is acceptable to you or fulfils a particular need or purpose.

Earth Again

1. How did the Tyrrans feel when they first got to Earth?

A. They felt overwhelmed by the size of everything.

B. They felt excited about all the attention they were receiving.

C. They felt comfortable being around big buildings and people.

D. They felt homesick because they were so far away from their planet.

2. What had the people of Earth prepared for the Tyrrans?

A. They had built a tennis court for the Tyrrans to play at.

B. They had constructed a village for the Tyrrans to live in.

C. They had created a spaceship for the Tyrrans to use.

D. They had set up houses that looked just like the ones on Tyrra.

3. What was true about TyrraVille Two?

A. It was not completed until after the *Star Scout* had landed.

B. It was located inside of the White House.

C. There was no public transportation system there.

D. The buildings and houses had come from toy stores.

4. What did the Lambchops do after saying good-bye to the Tyrrans?

A. They gave an interview to TV reporters.

B. They had dinner with the President.

C. They went home to rest.

D. They walked back to the *Star Scout* to sleep.

5. What did the Tyrrans eventually do?

A. They helped the people of Earth explore other planets.

B. They turned TyrraVille Two into a big city.

C. They decided to stay on Earth forever.

D. They returned to Tyrra.

Check Your Reading Speed
1분에 몇 단어를 읽는지 리딩 속도를 측정해보세요.

$$\frac{552 \text{ words}}{\text{reading time ( ) sec}} \times 60 = (\quad) \text{ WPM}$$

Build Your Vocabulary

⁑ pleasure [pléʒər] n. 기쁨, 즐거움
A pleasure is an activity, experience or aspect of something that you find very enjoyable or satisfying.

⁑ president [prézədənt] n. 대통령; 회장
The president of a country that has no king or queen is the person who is the head of state of that country.

⁑ lawn [lɔːn] n. 잔디밭, 잔디
A lawn is an area of grass that is kept cut short and is usually part of someone's garden or backyard, or part of a park.

⁎ reporter [ripɔ́ːrtər] n. (보도) 기자, 리포터
A reporter is someone who writes news articles or who broadcasts news reports.

⁑ tiny [táini] a. 아주 작은
Something or someone that is tiny is extremely small.

grandstand [grǽndstænd] n. 특별관람석
A grandstand is a covered stand with rows of seats for people to sit on at sporting events.

⁑ occasion [əkéiʒən] n. (특별한) 행사; 때, 기회
An occasion is an important event, ceremony, or celebration.

applaud [əplɔ́ːd] v. 박수를 치다; 갈채를 보내다
When a group of people applaud, they clap their hands in order to show approval, for example when they have enjoyed a play or concert.

polite [pəláit] a. 공손한, 정중한; 예의상의, 의례적인 (politely ad. 공손히, 예의 바르게)
Someone who is polite has good manners and behaves in a way that is socially correct and not rude to other people.

crowd [kraud] n. 사람들, 군중; v. 가득 메우다; (생각이 마음속에) 밀려오다
A crowd is a large group of people who have gathered together.

scout [skaut] n. 정찰병; 스카우트; v. (무엇을 찾아) 돌아다니다; 정찰하다
A scout is someone who is sent to an area of countryside to find out the position of an enemy army.

land [lænd] v. (땅·표면에) 내려앉다, 착륙하다; (땅에) 떨어지다; n. 육지, 땅; 지역
(landing n. 착륙)
A landing is an act of bringing an aircraft or spacecraft down to the ground.

be in store idiom ~이 기다리다; 준비되다
If something is in store for you, it is going to happen at some time in the future.

sheet [ʃiːt] n. (침대) 시트; (종이) 한 장
A sheet is a large rectangular piece of cotton or other cloth that you sleep on or cover yourself with in a bed.

spread [spred] v. (spread–spread) 펼치다; 퍼뜨리다, 확산시키다;
n. 스프레드(빵에 발라 먹는 식품); 확산, 전파
If you spread something somewhere, you open it out or arrange it over a place or surface, so that all of it can be seen or used easily.

signal [sígnəl] n. 신호; 징조; v. (동작·소리로) 신호를 보내다; 암시하다
A signal is a gesture, sound, or action which intended to give a particular message to the person who sees or hears it.

gasp [gæsp] n. 헉 하는 소리를 냄; v. 숨이 턱 막히다, 헉 하고 숨을 쉬다
A gasp is a short quick breath of air that you take in through your mouth, especially when you are surprised, shocked, or in pain.

court [kɔːrt] n. (테니스) 코트; 법정, 법원
A court is an area in which you play a game such as tennis, basketball, badminton, or squash.

entire [intáiər] a. 전체의, 온
You use entire when you want to emphasize that you are referring to the whole of something.

miniature [míniətʃər] a. 소형의, 작은; n. 축소모형
Miniature is used to describe something which is very small, especially a smaller version of something which is normally much bigger.

railway [réilwei] n. 철로, 철길
A railway is a route between two places along which trains travel on steel rails.

serve [səːrv] v. (상품·서비스를) 제공하다; (조직·국가 등을 위해) 일하다; (특정한 용도로) 쓰일 수 있다
If something serves people or an area, it provides them with something that they need.

principal [prínsəpəl] a. 주요한, 주된; n. 교장
Principal means first in order of importance.

rush [rʌʃ] a. 급한; 바쁜; v. 급히 움직이다; 서두르다; n. 혼잡, 분주함
A rush is a situation in which you need to go somewhere or do something very quickly.

deliver [dilívər] v. 배달하다; (연설·강연 등을) 하다 (delivery n. 배달)
Delivery or a delivery is the bringing of letters, parcels, or other goods to someone's house or to another place where they want them.

leading [líːdiŋ] a. 가장 중요한, 선두적인
The leading person or thing in a particular area is the one which is most important or successful.

explore [iksplɔ́ːr] v. 탐험하다, 탐사하다; 분석하다
If you explore a place, you travel around it to find out what it is like.

doorway [dɔ́ːrwèi] n. 출입구
A doorway is a space in a wall where a door opens and closes.

furniture [fɔ́ːrniʧər] n. 가구
Furniture consists of large objects such as tables, chairs, or beds that are used in a room for sitting or lying on or for putting things on or in.

hooray [huréi] int. 만세!
People sometimes shout 'hooray!' when they are very happy and excited about something.

cupboard [kʌ́bərd] n. 벽장; 찬장
A cupboard is a piece of furniture that has one or two doors, usually contains shelves, and is used to store things.

suit [suːt] n. 정장; (특정한 활동 때 입는) 옷; v. 어울리다; ~에게 편리하다
A man's suit consists of a jacket, trousers, and sometimes a waistcoat, all made from the same fabric.

underwear [ʌ́ndərwɛ̀ər] n. 속옷
Underwear is clothing such as vests and pants which you wear next to your skin under your other clothes.

kneel [niːl] v. (knelt–knelt) 무릎을 꿇다
When you kneel, you bend your legs so that your knees are touching the ground.

fingertip [fíŋgərtip] n. 손가락 끝
Your fingertips are the ends of your fingers.

farewell [fɛ̀ərwél] n. 작별 (인사); int. 안녕히 가세요
Farewell means the same as goodbye.

paralyze [pǽrəlàiz] v. 마비시키다; 무력하게 하다; 쓸모없게 하다
If someone is paralyzed by an accident or an illness, they have no feeling in their body, or in part of their body, and are unable to move.

^복_습 **sigh** [sai] v. 한숨을 쉬다, 한숨짓다; 탄식하듯 말하다; n. 한숨
When you sigh, you let out a deep breath, as a way of expressing feelings such as disappointment, tiredness, or pleasure.

^복_습 **conquer** [káŋkər] v. (다른 나라나 민족을) 정복하다; 이기다; 극복하다
If one country or group of people conquers another, they take complete control of their land.

^복_습 **folk** [fouk] n. (pl.) 여러분, 얘들아; (pl.) (일반적인) 사람들; (pl.) 부모
You can use folks as a term of address when you are talking to several people.

[*]_* **supper** [sápər] n. 저녁 식사, (가벼운) 만찬
Some people refer to the main meal eaten in the early part of the evening as supper.

^복_습 **tiring** [táiəriŋ] a. 피곤하게 하는, 피곤한
If you describe something as tiring, you mean that it makes you tired so that you want to rest or sleep.

bedtime [bédtàim] n. 취침 시간, 잠자리에 드는 시간
Your bedtime is the time when you usually go to bed.

_* **tuck** [tʌk] v. 단단히 덮어 주다; 집어 넣다; 밀어넣다; n. 주름, 단
(tuck in idiom ~에게 이불을 잘 덮어 주다)
If you tuck someone in, especially a child, you cover them comfortably in bed by pulling the covers around them.

^복_습 **chuckle** [ʧʌkl] v. 킬킬 웃다; 빙그레 웃다; n. 킬킬거림; 속으로 웃기
When you chuckle, you laugh quietly.

scary [skéəri] a. 무서운, 겁나는
Something that is scary is rather frightening.

^복_습 **protect** [prətékt] v. 보호하다, 지키다; 보장하다
To protect someone or something means to prevent them from being harmed or damaged.

drowsy [dráuzi] a. 졸리는, 꾸벅꾸벅 조는
If you feel drowsy, you feel sleepy and cannot think clearly.

in time idiom 이윽고
If you say that something will happen in time or given time, you mean that it will happen eventually, when a lot of time has passed.

farness [fáːrnis] n. 멀리 떨어짐; 아득함
Farness is the condition of being far off.

unknown [ʌnnóun] a. 알려지지 않은; 유명하지 않은
If something is unknown to you, you have no knowledge of it.

"우리를 만나러 올래요?
누구 듣고 있나요?"
멀고 먼 저 우주에서,
이제까지 책에서 언급되었던
그 어떤 행성이나 별보다
더 멀리 떨어진 곳에서,
질문이 도착했습니다.
몇 번이고 말이지요.
"우리를 만나러 올래요?
누구 듣고 있나요?"

1장 전화 통화

토요일 아침, 램찹 씨(Mr. Lambchop)와 램찹 부인(Mrs. Lambchop)은 부엌에서 벽지를 붙이고 있었습니다.

"좋지 않아요, 조지(George)?" 램찹 부인이 풀을 저으면서, 말했습니다. "흥분되는 일도 없고. 완벽하게 평범한 날이잖아요."

램찹 씨는 그녀가 바로 무엇을 의미하는지 알았습니다. 신나는 일은 종종 문제를 일으키곤 합니다. 그들의 아들, 스탠리(Stanley)의 몸 위로 한밤중에 게시판이 떨어지면서 그가 납작해졌던 것이, 예를 들면, 그런 일이지요. 스탠리가 다시 둥글게 돌아올 때까지 신나기도 했지만, 걱정스럽기도 했습니다. 그리고 요정이 방문하고, 소원을 들어주는 일

도 있었지요. 오, 정말 흥미로웠습니다! 하지만 요정이 그가 뛰쳐나온 램프로 돌아가기 전에 모든 소원은 취소되어야 했습니다.

"그래요, 여보." 램찹 씨가 벽지를 매끄럽게 매만졌습니다. "평범해요. 가장 좋은 날이에요."

거실에서는 스탠리 램찹과 그의 남동생, 아서(Arthur)가 TV에 나오는 톰 토드(Tom Toad) 만화를 보고 있었습니다. 운동을 좋아하는 토드가 수상 스키를 타다가 떨어지면서, 크게 물을 튀겼습니다. 아서는 너무 크게 웃어서 전화가 오는 소리를 듣지 못했지만, 스탠리가 그걸 받았습니다.

"램찹 씨네 집인가요?" 전화를 건 사람이 말했습니다. "미합중국의 대통령입니다. 전화를 받은 사람은 누구시죠?"

스탠리가 미소 지었습니다. "프랑스의 국왕입니다."

"프랑스에는 왕이 없어요. 이제는 말이에요."

"실례지만, 전 농담을 하기에는 몹시 바빠요." 스탠리가 TV에 시선을 고정했습니다. "제 동생과 전 톰 토드 쇼를 보고 있단 말이에요."

"그렇다면, 계속 보고 있어요, 어린 친구!" 전화를 건 사람이 전화를 끊은 바로 그때, 램찹 부부가 안으로 들어와

서 쇼의 나머지를 보려고 했습니다.

"있잖아요(Hey), 맞춰 보실래요?" 스탠리가 말했습니다.

"건초(Hay)는 말을 위한 거란다." 램찹 부인이 언제나 조심스러운 언행에 대해 신경쓰면서, 말했습니다. "얘야, 누가 전화한 거였니?"

스탠리가 웃었습니다. "미국 대통령이요!"

아서도 또한 웃음을 터뜨렸습니다.

"스탠리 형이 *자기가* 프랑스의 왕이라고 말했어요!"

톰 토드가 갑자기 TV 화면에서 사라졌고, 미국 국기가 나타났습니다. "여러분께 워싱턴 D.C.(Washington D.C.)에 있는 백악관(White House)에서 보내온 특별한 메시지를 전해드리겠습니다." 아나운서의 깊은 목소리가 말했습니다. "신사 숙녀 여러분, 미합중국의 대통령입니다!"

화면이 자신의 책상 뒤에 앉은, 매우 심각해 보이는, 대통령을 보여줬습니다.

"국민 여러분." 대통령이 말했습니다. "전 이 방송을 끊게 되어 죄송하게 생각합니다, 하지만 저 바깥에 있는 누군가는 제가 전화로 농담이나 하는 데 시간을 낭비할 수 없는 몹시 바쁜 사람이라는 것을 깨닫지 못하고 있네요. 전 제가 말하는 그 사람이—그리고 전 프랑스 국왕을 말하는 게 *아닙니다*!—그걸

기억하면 좋겠습니다. 고맙습니다. 이제 다시 토드 쇼가 계속될 겁니다.

여전히 수상 스키를 타고 있는, 톰 토드가 다시 TV에 나왔습니다.

"스탠리!" 램찹 부인이 외쳤습니다. "정말 프랑스 국왕이라고 말했구나!"

"맙소사!" 아서가 말했습니다. "스탠리 형이 교도소에 가게 될까요?"

"전화로 잘난 척하는 녀석이 되지 말라는 법은 없단다." 램찹 씨가 말했습니다. "아마도 있어야 할지도 모르겠구나."

전화벨이 울렸고, 그가 전화를 받았습니다. "조지 램찹입니다."

"좋아요!" 대통령이 말했습니다. "난 당신과 통화하려고 애썼습니다!"

"오, 이런!" 램찹 씨가 말했습니다. "부디 이해해주세—"

"잠깐. 당신이 한때 납작해져서, 신문에 사진이 실렸던 아들을 둔 사람 맞지요?"

"제 아들 스탠리입니다, 대통령님." 램찹 씨가 말하면서, 다른 가족들에게 누구와 통화하고 있는지 알렸습니다.

"난 확실히 해야만 했어요." 대통령이 말했습니다. "우리는 만나야겠어요, 램찹 씨! 내가 즉시 내 개인 전용기를 보내서, 당신 모두를 여기 워싱턴 D.C.로 데려오도록 하겠어요."

램찹 씨가 숨을 혁 하고 들이마셨습니다. "개인 전용기라고요? 워싱턴에?

우리 모두를요?"

"가족 전부를 말이에요." 대통령이 껄껄 웃었습니다. "프랑스의 국왕도 함께요."

2장 워싱턴

백악관에 있는, 그의 유명한 대통령 집무실에서, 대통령은 모든 램찹 가족과 악수했습니다.

"와 줘서 고마워요." 그가 껄껄 웃었습니다. "여러분이 오늘 아침 일어났을 때 나를 만나게 될 거라고는 결코 생각하지 못했을 겁니다."

"정말 생각하지 못했죠." 램찹 씨가 말했습니다. "이건 상당히 놀라운 일이에요."

"흠, 그럴 일이 하나 더 있어요." 대통령이 말했습니다. "내가 여러분을 오라고 요청한 이유이기도 하지요."

그는 이제 진지해져서, 자기 책상 뒤에 앉았습니다. "티라(Tyrra)! 그것에 대해 들어본 적 없죠, 그렇죠?"

램찹 가족은 모두 고개를 저었습니다.

"아무도 여태까지 그것에 대해 들어보지 못했어요. 그건 저 위 어딘가에 있는 행성입니다. 그들이 메시지를 보냈어요, 저 우주에서 온 첫 번째 메시지를요!"

램찹 가족은 매우 흥미를 느꼈습니다. "상상해 보세요!" 램찹 부인이 외쳤습니다. "뭐라고 말하던가요?"

"아주 상냥한 어조였어요." 대통령이 말했습니다. "평화로운 분위기에, 그냥 확인하는 거였어요. 우리에게 방문해달라고 하더군요. 자, 내 계획은—"

집무실의 옆문이 갑자기 열리면서 잘 차려입고 왕관을 쓴 여성이 모습을 드러냈습니다. 램찹 부인은 즉시 그녀가 영국의 여왕이라는 것을 알아차렸습니다.

"연회에 관해서는, 또한 그—" 여왕이 말하기 시작하다가, 대통령이 바쁘다는 것을 보았습니다. "이런! 실례할게요." 그녀가 문을 닫았습니다.

"이곳은 *아수라장*이에요." 대통령이 말했습니다. "방문객들, 고급 만찬들, 끝이 없어요. 자, 어디까지 했더라—? 아, 그래요! 스타 스카우트(Star Scout)!"

그가 앞으로 몸을 내밀었습니다.

"그건 우리의 새 일급비밀 우주선입니다, 지금 막 준비됐어요! 난 생각했지요, 누군가를 스타 스카우트에 태워 보내, 이 티라인(Tyrran)들을 만나게 하자고 말이에요. 하지만 누구를 보내죠? 군인이나 과학자를 보내는 것은 평화로워 보이지 않을 거예요. 그래서 난 생각했습니다: 그냥 평범한 미국 소년보다 더 평화롭게 보이는 게 뭐가 있겠어요?"

대통령이 미소 지었습니다. "스탠리 램찹이라면 어떨까요?"

"스탠리를요?" 램찹 부인이 헉 하고 숨을 뱉었습니다. "우주선에 태워서요? 외계 종족을 만나기 위해서요?"

"오, 이럴 수가!" 스탠리가 말했습니다. "전 정말 가고 싶어요!"

"저도요." 아서가 말했습니다. "그건 공평하지 않아요, 만약에—"

"아서!" 램찹 씨가 크게 숨을 쉬었습니다. "대통령님, 왜 스탠리인가요?"

"이미 모험을 한 경험이 있는 사람이어야만 해요." 대통령이 말했습니다. "뭐, 내 경호팀이 스탠리가 납작해지고 도둑 두 명을 잡았을 때를 다룬 신문 기사를 내게 보여줬지요. 도둑이라니! 그건 모험이잖아요!"

"저도 그런 경험이 있어요!" 아서가 말했습니다. "요정이 제게 나는 법을 가르쳐 주었고, 우린 사자코끼리 (Liophant)도 있었고, 또—"

"뭐가 있었다고?"

"사자코끼리요." 아서가 말했습니다. "반은 사자이고, 반은 코끼리의 모습을 했어요. 그것들은 좋았어요."

"그러니? 경호팀은 결코—"

"대통령님?" 램찹 부인은 말을 끊고 싶지 않았지만, 그녀의 걱정이 컸습니다. "대통령님?" 그녀가 말했습니다. "이

우주 비행 말인데요: 안전한가요?"

"세상에, 물론 안전하지요!" 대통령이 말했습니다. "우리는 많은 주의를 기울였어요, 램찹 부인. 스타 스카우트는 모든 최신 과학 설비를 갖추고 있습니다. 그리고 매우 조심스럽게 시험을 거쳤습니다. 우선, 우리는 승객 없이, 자동 조종으로 그것을 시험해 보았습니다. 그건 완벽하게 운행했지요! 심지어 그러고 나서도, 부인, 우리는 만족하지 않았어요. 우리는 스타 스카우트를 다시 쏘아 올렸습니다. 이번에는 우리의 가장 똑똑하고 훈련받은 새를 태워서 말이지요. 그런데 직접 들어보세요." 대통령이 자기 책상 위에 있는 작은 상자에 대고 말했습니다. "슈워츠 박사(Dr. Schwartz)를 들여 보내주세요."

턱수염이 난 남자가 하얀 코트를 입고 위에 천을 씌운 새장을 들고서, 들어왔습니다. 허리를 살짝 굽혀 인사를 하더니, 그가 천을 걷어 크고, 선명한 형형색색의 앵무새를 드러냈습니다.

"고맙소, 허만(Herman)." 대통령이 말했습니다. "슈워츠 박사는 우리의 최고 우주 과학자입니다." 그가 램찹 가족에게 말했습니다. "그리고 이건 폴리 (Polly), 내가 말했던 새입니다. 폴리, 여기 이분들에게 네가 우주로 갔던 모험에 대해 이야기해주렴."

"식은 죽 먹기." 앵무새가 말했습니다.

"멋졌어요! 매 순간이 좋았어요!"

"고마워요, 허만." 대통령이 말했고 슈워츠 박사가 폴리를 데리고 갔습니다.

"저건 매우 안심되지만, 스탠리가 혼자 간다는 건 말이 안 돼요." 램찹 부인이 말했습니다. "하지만, 우리는 가족 휴가를 가려고 했어요. 그게 가능할까요, 대통령님, 우리 모두 가는 게 말이에요?"

"뭐, 여러분이 너무 좁은 것을 신경 쓰지 않는다면요." 대통령이 말했습니다. "그리고 짐을 덜 챙기는 게 상관없다면요."

"사실, 우리는 해변에 가는 걸 염두에 두고 있었죠." 램찹 씨가 말했습니다. "아니면 테니스 캠프라든지. 하지만—"

영국 여왕이 다시 안을 들여다보았습니다. "물어봐도 될까—"

"잠깐 기다려요, 맙소사!" 대통령이 말했습니다.

"우리가 곧 돌아오지요." 짜증이 난 것처럼 보이면서, 여왕이 가 버렸습니다.

램찹 씨가 결정했습니다. "대통령님, 해변은 기다릴 수 있어요. 우리는 티라로 가겠습니다, 대통령님."

"훌륭해요!" 대통령이 벌떡 일어났습니다. "별들을 향해서 가세요, 램찹 가족들! 우주 센터에서 약간의 훈련을 받고 나면, 여러분은 떠날 수 있을 겁니다!"

3장 이륙

"10!" 관제 센터에서 나는 목소리가 말했습니다.

카운트다운이 시작되었습니다. 그게 "0"에 다다르면, 주조종사 스탠리 램찹이 "출발" 단추를 누를 것이고, 스타 스카우트는 티라를 향해 발사될 것입니다.

"9!"

자신들의 자리에서 벨트를 차고서, 램찹 가족은 숨을 죽인 채, 각자 매우 다른 생각들을 하고 있었습니다.

스탠리는 티라인들이 지구에서 단지 평범한 가족을 보냈다는 것을 신경 쓸지 궁금해했습니다. 만약 그들이 엄청 거만한 사람들이고 장군이나 TV 스타, 또는 대통령이 오기를 기대했다면? 만약에— "8!" 관제 센터가 말했고, 스탠리는 자신의 두 눈을 자기 앞에 있는 계기판에 고정했습니다.

램찹 씨는 자신의 국가를 위해 봉사하는 것은 명예로운 일이지만 이건 좀 지나치다고 생각하고 있었습니다. 어떻게 이런 일들이 일어나는 걸까요? 정체를 알 수 없는 행성으로, 온 식구가 떠나다니! 다른 가족은 납작해지는 아들을 두고 있지 않습니다. 다른 가족은 집에서 요정을 발견하지도 않지요. 다른—오, 어쩌겠어요! 램찹 씨가 한숨을 쉬었습니다.

"7!" 관제 센터가 말했습니다.

램찹 부인은 램찹 씨가 조바심을 내는 것 같다고 생각했습니다. 하지만 왜 그럴까요, 이제 스타 스카우트가 이렇게 멋지게 보이는데 말이에요? 사실, 그녀 덕분이지요. "그들은 그것을 우주선(spaceship)이라고 부르겠지요." 그녀가 그것을 처음 보았을 때 말했습니다. "하지만 공간(space)이 어디에 있다는 거죠? 그냥 방 하나일 뿐이잖아요! 그리고 모두 회색이라니 . . . ? 어머나, 칙칙해라!" 그러나, 우주 센터에서 이뤄진 훈련 대부분은 신체 운동이었고, 램찹 부인은, 규칙적으로 조깅을 하고 운동을 했기에, 요구된 시험을 빠르게 통과했습니다. 그 후 며칠간, 다른 가족들이 몸을 만드는 동안에, 그녀는 자신의 자유 시간을 활용해 스타 스카우트를 좀 더 집처럼 꾸몄습니다. 허용된 무게는 그다지 많지 않았지만, 그녀는 샤워실에 둘 욕실용 체중계와 비닐 커튼, 둥근 창에 달 예쁜 블라인드, 돋보기가 달린 탐색창에 달 베니션 블라인드(venetian blind), 그리고 멕시코와 프랑스 포스터를 용케 넣었습니다.

"6! . . . 5! . . . 4! . . . 3! . . ."

램찹 부인은 자기 가방이 그녀의 자리 밑에 잘 들어가 있는지 확인했습니다.

아서는, 선천적으로 게을렀는데, 자신이 그 모든 조깅하고, 뛰고, 사다리를 올라가고, 벽을 오르는 훈련을 끝내서 기뻤습니다. 그가, 요정 덕분에, 엄청 강했을 땐, 그건 쉬웠을 겁니다. 하지만 그냥 평범한 아서 램찹에게는, 그가 생각했을 때, 그건 피곤한 일이었습니다.

"2!" 관제 센터가 말했습니다. "행운을 빌어요, 모두! 1!"

"집중하렴, 얘야." 램찹 부인이 스탠리에게 말했습니다.

"0!" 관제 센터가 말했고, 스탠리는 "출발" 단추를 눌렀습니다.

부우웅! 로켓이 굉음을 내면서, 스타 스카우트가 그 발사대에서 이륙했습니다.

부우우우웅! 부우우우웅! 속도를 내면서, 그건 점점 더 높이 하늘로 치솟으며, 램찹 가족을 티라 행성이 있는 저먼 곳으로 보냈습니다.

4장 우주에서

"난 이 오믈렛을 뒤집기만 하면 돼." 스타 스카우트에서 아침 식사를 준비하면서, 램찹 부인이 말했습니다. "그러고 나서― 오, 이런!" 오믈렛이 그녀 위 허공에서 마치 프리스비(Frisbee)처럼 떠 있었습니다.

하지만, 대부분은, 우주에서 몇 주를

보내고 나니, 램찹 가족은, 물건들을 아래로 당기는 힘, 중력이 지구의 대기권 밖에서는 존재하지 않는다는 것을 기억했습니다. 램찹 씨는 이제 종종 자기 머리 뒤로 두 손을 깍지 낀 채 읽으면서, 자기 몸 앞에 자신의 책이 둥둥 떠 있게 두곤 했고, 스탠리과 아서는 자기 자리에서 밀듯이 일어나서 방을 가로지르며 깃털처럼 떠다니는 것을 아주 즐겼습니다.

그녀의 프라이팬을 들어 올려서, 램찹 부인은 오믈렛을 아래로 내렸습니다. "아침 식사를 한 뒤에는, 무엇을 하지?" 그녀가 말했습니다. "모노폴리(Monopoly) 게임을 할까?"

"제발, 또 하지는 말아요." 아서가 한숨 쉬었습니다. "만약에 이 모험이 이렇게 지루할 줄 알았다면, 저는 절대로 오지 않았을 거예요."

"최악인 건." 스탠리가 말했습니다. "그게 얼마나 오래 지속될지 모른다는 점이에요."

"시작할 때는 지루하지 않았어요." 아서가 말하면서 그들은 아침 식사를 하기 시작했습니다. "출발할 때는 재미있었어요."

처음 며칠은 사실 무척이나 흥미진진했습니다. 그들은 스타 스카우트의 돋보기 창문에서 많은 시간을 보내며, 선명한 지구가 점차 작아지다가, 결국에는 단지 까만 우주 속 색이 옅은 유리구슬처럼 보일 때까지 지켜보았습니다. 그리고 많은 특이한 볼 것들: 별이 쏟아질 듯한 아름다움을 지닌 은하수(Milky Way), 행성들—붉은 화성(Mars), 거대한 목성(Jupiter), 구름으로 덮인 금성(Venus), 빛나는 고리를 가진 토성(Saturn)이 있었습니다.

3일째 저녁에는 그들은 지구에서 방송되는 TV 뉴스에 나왔습니다. 그들의 여행에 대한 정보가 언론에 공개되었고, 전 세계에서 사람들이 이 독특한 모험이 어떻게 진행되고 있는지 간절하게 알고 싶어 했습니다. 우주선의 카메라 앞에 서서, 램찹 가족은 그들이 괜찮으며, 타 라인들을 만나기를 기대하고 있고, 그들이 TV 송신 범위 내에 있는 동안 밤마다 소식을 알리겠다고 말했습니다.

4일째 저녁에 그들은 카메라 앞에서 떠다니면서, 무중력 상태를 보여주었습니다. 이는 지구에서 대단히 호응이 좋아서, 그들은 다음 날에 또 떠 있었습니다.

그러나, 6일째 저녁이 되자, 그들은 자신들이 방송에 나오는 모습을 활기차게 꾸미느라 애를 먹었습니다. 램찹 씨는 야구 시, "타석에 선 케이시(Casey at the Bat)"를 낭송했습니다. 스탠리는 테니스공으로 저글링을 했는데, 지구 시청자들은, 이제 무중력 상태에 대해 알기에, 그가 그것들을 위로 던졌을 때 공들이 떠 있는 것을 보았습니다. 아서는 수탉, 개, 그리고 전화 부스에 갇힌 남자 흉내를 냈습니다. 이 다음에, 램참 부인이 그녀의 대학교 교가를 부르는 동안에, 그는 샤워하려고 비닐 커튼 뒤에서 옷을 벗다가 실수로 커튼을 잡아당기고 말았습니다. 그는 창피해했고, 그녀가 나중에 그를 위로하려고 했습니다.

"우리는 기억될 거란다, 아서, 우주에서 보낸 우리의 시간 때문에 말이야." 그녀가 말했습니다. "누구도 커튼 따위에 신경 쓰지 않는단다."

"전 영원히 기억될 거예요." 아서가 말했습니다. "수백만 명의 사람들이 속옷만 입은 제 모습을 봤다고요."

다음 날은 스탠리의 생일이었고, 저녁 식사 직후에 화면이 켜졌습니다. 거기에는 셔츠 차림의 대통령이, 워싱턴 D.C.에 있는 자신의 책상 뒤에 있었습니다.

"흠, 나는 또 늦게까지 이렇게 일하고 있어요." 대통령이 말했습니다. "어려운 직업이에요, 내 말을 믿어요. 생일 축하한다, 스탠리 램참! 난 깜짝 선물을 준비했단다. 먼저, 네 학교 친구들이야."

잠시 흐르던 침묵이, 목을 가다듬는 소리에 깨졌고, 그리고 나서, 수백만 마일 떨어진 곳에서, 스탠리의 학급 친구들이 노래하는 소리가 들렸습니다. "생일 축하합니다, 사랑하는 스탠리! 생일 축하합니다!"

스탠리는 굉장히 기뻐했습니다. "고마워, 모두!" 그가 말했습니다. "고맙습니다, 대통령님."

"저건 단지 미국이 맡은 부분일 뿐이란다." 대통령이 말했습니다. "거기 런던에서는 준비되었나요, 여왕님?"

"우리는 준비되었어요." 여왕의 목소리가 유쾌하게 말했습니다. "그리고 자, 램참 군, 우리의 유명한 웨스트민스터(Westminster) 소년 합창단이에요!"

영국에서, 유명한 합창단이 내는 아름다운 목소리로 "생일 축하합니다, 스탠리!"라고 다시 한 번 노래를 불렀고, 그다음에는 독일, 스페인, 그리고 프랑스에서 다른 아이들이 노래를 불렀습니다.

스탠리에게 쏟아지는 이 모든 관심에 아서가 시샘했고, 그때 대통령이 말했습니다. "그건 그렇고, 아서, 네가 우리를 지난밤에 아주 재미있게 해주었단다." 그는 이것이 속옷을 입은 자신의 모습에 대한 장난이라고 확신했습니다. 하지만 그가 틀렸습니다.

"그 흉내들이란!" 대통령이 말했습니다. "특히 전화 부스에 있는 남자 말이야. 미친 듯이 좋았어!"

"정말이야!" 여왕이 영국에서 덧붙였습니다. "우리는 매우 즐거웠단다."

"오, 고마워요!" 아서가 환호하며, 말했습니다. "전—"

화면이 꺼졌습니다.

그들이 너무 멀리 나왔습니다. 지구에서 오는 목소리도 더는 없고, 티라인이 뭐라고 말할지 듣기 전까지는 그들 자신의 목소리 외에는 아무 소리도 없었습니다.

"만약에 티라인들이 우리가 오는 것을 잊어버렸다면요?" 스탠리가 말했습니다. "우리는 영원히 우주에서 항해를 해야 할 수도 있어요."

그들은 아침 식사로 오믈렛을 다 먹었고, 이제는 모노폴리 게임판을 펼치고 있었는데 왜냐하면 할 만한 더 흥미로운 일이 없었기 때문입니다.

"그들은 심지어 우리 이름도 모르잖아요." 아서가 말했습니다. "그들이 우리를 뭐라고 부를까요?"

"지구인들!" 낮은 목소리가 말했습니다.

"매우 그럴듯하구나." 램찹 씨가 말했습니다. "'지구인들'은 보기에— 누가 말한 거니?"

"난 아니에요(Not me)." 스탠리와 아서 둘 다 말했습니다.

"전 아니에요(Not I), 라고 해야지." 말을 고치면서, 램찹 부인이 말했습니다. "하지만 누가—"

"지구인들!" 목소리가, 이제는 더 크게, 스타 스카우트의 무전을 통해 나왔습니다. "위대한 행성 티라와 그곳의 훌륭한 사람들이 안부를 전합니다! 잘 들리나요?"

"오, 이런!" 램찹 씨가 소리를 키웠습니다. "그것들(them)이잖아!"

"그 사람들(They)이라고 해야죠." 램찹 부인이 말했습니다.

"세상에 맙소사, 해리엇(Harriet)!" 램찹 씨가 말했고, 마이크에 대고 크게 말했습니다. "안녕하세요, 티라. 지구인들입니다. 인원은 총 4명입니다. 평화를 사랑하는 가족이지요."

"평화를 사랑한다고?" 목소리가 말했습니다. "좋아요! 위대한 티라도 그렇답니다! 어디에 있나요, 지구인들?"

스탠리는 자신의 항성 지도를 확인했습니다. "우리는 랠프 혜성(Ralph's Comet)의 끝부분이 삼백만 사십칠 번 별과 만나는 바로 그곳에 있어요. 이제 어떡하죠?"

"알겠어요." 티라인의 목소리가 말했습니다. "여러분이 꼭 발처럼 생긴 별자리를 지나갈 때까지 계속 가세요. 여러분은 놓치지 않을 겁니다. 그다음, 살짝 한쪽으로 기운 하얀 달을 지나가자마자, 내려오기 시작하세요. 여러분은 뾰족한 산, 그다음엔 큰 들판을 보게 될 겁니다. 거기에 착륙해요. 곧 만납시다,

지구인들!"

"당연하죠!" 램찹 씨가 말했고, 그의 가족에게 돌아섰습니다. "다른 행성과 첫 번째 만남이라니! 우리가 역사를 쓰고 있다고!"

그들은 발 모양의 별자리를 지났고, 그다음에는 한쪽으로 기울어진 달을 지나, 그리고 스탠리는 스타 스카우트를 착륙하도록 조종했습니다. 그것이 내려가면서 우주의 어둠은 사라졌고, 마침내 램찹 가족은 도착하기까지 그렇게나 오래 걸렸던 행성을 분명하게 보게 되었습니다.

티라는 행성치고는 작았지만, 지구의 바다와 대륙과는 그다지 다르지 않은 특징이 있고 모두 갈색의 색조를 띠었으며, 정확히 둥글고 꽤 아름다웠습니다. 뾰족한 산이 시야에 들어왔고, 그 뒤에 넓은 들판이 있었습니다.

"저기예요!" 스탠리가 "착륙" 단추를 눌렀습니다.

부우웅! 스타 스카우트의 로켓이 작동했습니다. 우주선이 공중을 맴돌다가, 착륙했습니다.

밖을 내다보니, 램찹 가족은 단지 황갈색의 나무들이 한편에 있고 약간 갈색을 띤 언덕이 그 너머에 있는 갈색 들판만을 보았습니다.

"흥미롭구나." 램찹 씨가 말했습니다. "어디에—"

갑자기 메시지가 왔지만, 그들이 기대하던 종류는 아니었습니다.

"항복하라, 지구인들!" 무전에서 말했습니다. "너희 우주선은 우리의 끊을 수 없는 함정 밧줄에 의해 붙잡혀 있다! 너희는 티라의 포로다! 항복하라!"

5장 티라인

끊을 수 없는 함정 밧줄? 포로? 항복하라고? 램찹 가족은 자신들이 제대로 듣고 있는지 믿을 수가 없었습니다.

"난 저걸 평화롭다고 부르지는 않겠어요." 램찹 부인이 말했습니다. "우리 대통령이 속았어요."

"난 우리가 해변에 갔더라면 좋았겠어요." 램찹 씨가 고개를 저었습니다. "하지만 어떻게 우리가 갇혀 있는 걸까요? 난 모르—" 그가 확대 창문을 가리켰습니다. "저게 뭐지?"

실 같은, 가느다란 파란 선이 스타 스카우트를 가로질러 지나가고 있었습니다. 스탠리는 유리창 닦개를 큰 창문 위로 지나가게 작동시켰고 그 날이 한 번 지나가자 파란 선이 끊어졌습니다.

"젠장(Drat)!" 무전에서 말했습니다.

다른 목소리가 깜짝 놀라며, 높아졌고, 그러더니 낮은 목소리가 다시 말했습니다. "지구인들이여! 우리가 특사를 보내도록 하겠소! 보통의, 평범한 티라인으로, 우리가 어떻게 생겼는지 보여주려는 것뿐입니다."

한참 동안, 램찹 가족은 들판 건너편의 황갈색 나무들에 시선을 고정했습니다.

"저기!" 아서가 갑자기 말했습니다. "오고 있어요— 오! 오, 이런 . . ." 그의 목소리가 잦아들었습니다.

티라인 특사가 천천히 다가와 큰 창문 앞에 섰는데, 우락부락하고, 얼굴을 찌푸리고 돌돌 말린 콧수염을 단 젊은 남자가, 반바지를 입고 몽둥이를 들고 있었습니다.

그 콧수염은 몹시 컸습니다. 특사는 그렇지 않았지요.

"저 남자는." 램찹 부인이 천천히 말했습니다. "고작 3인치(3 inches, 7.62센티미터)정도 밖에 되지 않아요."

"기껏해야 말이죠." 램찹 씨가 말했습니다. "확대 창문이잖아요."

그 티라인이 무언가를 외치고 있는 듯했습니다. 아서는 문을 아주 조금 열었고, 그 말이 이제 분명하게 들렸습니다. ". . . 우리가 너희의 모습을 보는 걸 두려워하고 있나, 지구인들? 내가 너무 거대해서? 하! 모든 티라인이 이렇게 크다고!"

문을 크게 벌컥 열면서, 아서가 자신의 모습을 드러냈습니다. "글쎄, 난 작은 지구인이에요!" 그가 소리쳤습니다. "나머지 사람은 나(me)보다 훨씬 더 크다고요!"

"저(I)라고 해야지, 나(me)라고 하지 말고." 램찹 부인이 말했습니다. "그리고 장난치지 말렴, 아스— 오! 그가 기절했어!"

그녀의 손수건을 차가운 물로 적셔서, 그녀는 스타 스카우트에서 뛰어 내려갔고 달려가 그 티라인의 아주 작은 이마를 가볍게 눌러 닦았습니다.

울음소리가 우주선의 무전기에서 다시 높아졌습니다. "거인이 익크(Ik)를 죽였어! . . . 또 다른, 훨씬 더 큰 사람이 있어! . . . 오, 끔찍해! . . . 봐! 익크가 괜찮아!"

그 티라인은, 램찹 부인의 손수건을 붙잡아서, 실제로 자기 몸을 일으켰습니다. 화를 내며, 그는 자신의 곤봉을 휘둘렀지만, 단지 그녀의 신발코를 두드렸을 뿐이었습니다. "아악! 저리 가!" 그녀가 말했고, 그는 황급히 들판을 가로질러 돌아갔습니다.

"오, 맙소사!" 무전기에서 말했습니다. "항복하는 건 잊어버려요, 지구인들! 휴전 위원회가 가고 있어요!"

처음에는 그들은 단지 조그마한 깃발이, 갈색 들판 저편에서 마치 하얀 나비처럼 펄럭이는 모습만을 보았지만, 마침

내 티라인 휴전 위원회가 가까이 다가왔고, 이제 스타 스카우트 밖에서 기다리고 있는, 램찹 가족은 키가 작은 사람들 각자를 볼 수 있었습니다.

깃발은 인상을 찌푸린 그 콧수염이 있고 곤봉을 든 젊은 남자가 들고 있었습니다. 그보다도 조금 더 작은, 위원회의 다른 사람들은, 가슴에 메달들이 달린 군복을 입은 얼굴이 붉은 남자, 노란 드레스를 입고 꽃이 달린 모자를 쓴 통통한 여자, 그리고 푸른 정장을 입은 더 나이가 많은 두 남자로 이루어졌는데, 한 사람은 구불구불한 흰 머리카락을 가졌고, 다른 사람은 마르고 대머리였습니다.

위원회는 멈춰서, 용감하게 위를 쳐다보았습니다.

"난 앱(Ap) 장군이오!" 군복을 입은 남자가 소리쳤습니다. "모든 티라 군대의 지휘관입니다!"

스탠리가 앞으로 나섰습니다. "주조종사 스탠리 램찹입니다." 그가 말했습니다. "지구에서 왔어요. 이분들은 제 부모님, 조지 램찹 부부입니다. 그리고 제 동생, 아서예요."

"티라의 오트(Ot) 대통령과 오트 부인(Mrs. Ot)입니다." 앱 장군이 말하면서, 구불거리는 머리카락을 가진 남자와 여자를 가리켰습니다. "대머리인 남자는 엡 박사(Dr. Ep)으로, 우리 과학자

입니다. 국기를 들고 투덜거리는 사람이 내 부하, 익크 대위입니다."

아무도 그다음에 무슨 말을 해야 할지 확신하지 못하는 듯했습니다. 몇몇 공손한 말들이 오갔는데—"만나서 반가워요, 지구인들!"... "티라는 정말 아름다운 행성이네요!"... "고마워요, 우주에서 아주 오래 있었나요?"—그리고 램찹 씨가 문득 티라인들이 계속 고개를 위로 거의 바싹 치켜든 채 이야기하는 것이 불편하리란 걸 알아차렸습니다. 그가 자신의 무릎을 꿇자, 다른 램찹 가족도 그의 행동을 따라 했고, 티라인들이 그 즉시 안도하며 자신들의 고개를 내렸습니다.

"좋아요!" 앱 장군이 말했습니다. "모두 합리적인 사람이네요! 휴전합시다, 응?"

"솔직히, 난 전쟁이 더 낫다고 봐요." 익크 대위가 으르렁거리듯 말했지만, 스탠리는 듣지 못한 척했습니다. "휴전이요? 좋은 생각이에요." 그가 말했습니다. "우리는 싸우려고 온 게 아니에요."

오트 부인이 코웃음을 쳤습니다. "그다지 평화롭지는 않네요, 불쌍한 익크 대위를 놀라게 한 걸 보면." 그녀가 아서를 가리켰습니다. "저 거인이 그에게 소리쳤잖아요!"

"내 아들은 거인이 아니에요." 램찹 부인이 말했습니다. "단지 여러분 티라

인들이—뭐라고 말해야 하나?—대단히 체격이 작을 뿐이에요."

"익크는 우리 중에 제일 큰 사람이에요, 사실." 앱 장군이 말했습니다. "우리는 그가 당신들을 겁주기를 바랐죠."

오트 대통령이 그의 손을 들었습니다. "어떠한 피해도 없었어요! 오세요! 티라빌(TyrraVille), 우리의 수도는 조금만 더 걸어가면 됩니다."

램찹 가족은 이제 스타 스카우트의 과학 도구함에서 꺼낸 휴대용 돋보기 렌즈를 가지고, 위원회를 따라갔습니다.

티라빌은 황갈색 나무 뒤편으로, 갈색 들판 바로 건너편에 펼쳐져 있었는데, 지구의 테니스 코트 크기 정도 밖에 되지 않았습니다.

6장 티라빌

"맙소사!" 스탠리가 말했습니다. "어떤 면에서, 고향 생각이 나게 하네요."

그 크기가 다르고 녹색이 없다는 것만을 제외한다면, 티라의 수도는 정말 지구의 작은 마을과 똑 닮았습니다. 중심가는 쇼핑하고 볼일을 보러 다니는 사람들로 북적였습니다; 보기 좋은 학교와 공공건물들, 램찹 씨의 허리 높이까지 오는 첨탑이 있는 두 교회, 그리고 아기자기한 갈색 우표 같은 잔디가 있는 예쁜 집들이 놓인 골목들이 있었습니다.

익크 대위는, 여전히 화가 나서, 앞장서서 급히 걸어갔지만, 위원회의 나머지 사람들은 중심가의 입구에서 멈춰 섰습니다.

"우리가 여러분에게 주변을 구경시켜 줄게요, 응?" 오트 대통령이 말했습니다. "내 생각에는, 그게 더 안전하겠어요."

램찹 가족은 즉시 자신들의 발보다 겨우 조금 넓은 거리를 걸어다니는 것이 위험하다는 걸 알아차렸습니다. 위원회의 인도를 받으며, 그들은 작은 수도를 빙빙 돌면서, 종종 그들의 돋보기 렌즈를 사용해 허리를 굽혀서 보기도 했습니다. 오트 부인은 특별히 흥미로운 것들을 가리키는 데 신경을 썼는데, 그중에는 억스(Ux) 들판, 스포츠 센터, 억스 제독 광장, 억스 공원, 그리고 억스 과학 센터 건물이 있었습니다. ("오트 부인의 할아버지는." 앱 장군이 속삭였습니다. "매우 부유했지요!")

그 관광은 큰 소동을 일으켰습니다. 사방에서 티라빌의 작은 시민들이 창문과 옥상에서 손을 흔들었습니다. 마지막 도착지, 과학 센터에서는, 기자들이 사진을 찍었고, 램찹 가족은 티라의 국가적 음료, 포도 맛 피졸라(Grape Fizzola)를 대접받았는데, 지구인에게 맞는 1인분의 양을 맞추느라 수백 병을

4개의 통에 비워 담아야만 했습니다.

자신의 피졸라를 마시고 기운을 낸, 아서가 조금 달려서 티라빌의 넓은 부분을 뛰어넘었고, 억스 광장에 착지했습니다. "아서!" 램찹 부인이 꾸중했고, 그가 다시 뛰어넘어 돌아왔습니다.

"아이들은 개구쟁이지 않나요?" 한 티라인 엄마가 구경하면서, 말했습니다. "내 아이는―그만 잡아당기렴, 허버트(Herbert)!" 이 마지막 말은 그녀 옆의 땅에다가 하는 듯했습니다. "내 막내예요." 그녀가 설명했습니다.

스탠리가 눈을 가늘게 뜨고 보았습니다. "전 거의 볼 수 없―그는 그냥 점 같이 작아요."

"네가 더 꼬마야!" 화가 난 목소리가 말했습니다. "이 키만 큰 녀석아! 네가 웃기게 생긴 놈이라고!"

"허버트!" 그의 엄마가 말했습니다. "사람들의 체형이나 크기를 가지고 놀리는 것은 무례한 짓이야!"

"저도 그렇게 자주 말하곤 했어요, 스탠리가 납작했을 때 말이에요!" 램찹 부인이 외쳤습니다. "그랬다면 좋았을―"

"항복해라, 지구인들아!"

그 외침은 익크 대위에게서 나온 것이었는데, 그는 이제 과학 센터 뒤에서 모습을 드러내며, 거의 그 자신만큼이나 크고, 관이 툭 튀어나온, 상자 같은 기계의 무게에 휘청거렸습니다.

"항복해!" 그가 외쳤습니다. "너희는 우리의 마그노-타이타닉 마비 광선(Magno-Titanic Paralyzer Ray)을 이겨낼 수 없을 것이다! 티라는 이제 살 수 있을 것이다!"

"휴전 중이잖아, 익크!" 앱 장군이 소리 질렀습니다. "넌 그러면 안―"

"난 그럴 수 있어요! 먼저― 앗!" 익크 대위의 무릎이 꺾였지만, 그는 자신의 몸을 바로 했습니다. "먼저 나는 저 들판에서 나를 놀라게 했던 녀석을 마비시킬 겁니다!"

마그노-타이타닉 마비총에서 나오는 노란빛이 아서를 향해 깜빡거렸습니다.

"이키!" 아서가 말했고, 사람들 사이에서 비명이 나왔습니다.

하지만 마그노-타이타닉 광선에 맞은 것은 아서가 아니었습니다. 스탠리가 자신의 동생을 보호하려고 앞으로 뛰쳐나왔고, 그 빛은 이제 그의 가슴과 어깨 위에서 빛을 냈습니다. 램찹 부인은 실신할 지경이었습니다.

갑자기 그녀의 두려움이 사라졌습니다.

스탠리는 미소 짓고 있었습니다. 노란 광선이 여전히 그의 몸 위에서 번쩍이는 와중에, 그는 자신의 고개를 돌렸고 자신의 손을 꿈틀꿈틀 움직여 그가 괜찮다는 것을 보였습니다. "괜찮은 기분이에요, 사실은." 그가 말했습니다. "마치

마사지를 받는 것 같아요."

사람들이 환호했습니다. "그건 단지 티라인-크기의 사람들에게만 효과가 있는 거야!" 누군가가 외쳤습니다. "당신은 멍청이야, 익크!" 그리고는 익크 대위는 티라 경찰에 의해 끌려갔고, 사람들은 여전히 웃으면서, 흩어졌습니다.

램참 부인은 위원회에 단호하게 말했습니다. "'티라는 이제 구해질 것이다'라고요? 익크 대위가 한 말이 무슨 뜻이지요? 그리고, 부디 말해주세요, 왜 그가 내 아들을 마비시키려고 했던 건가요?"

오트 부부와 앱 장군은 시선을 주고받았습니다. 엡 박사는 땅을 쳐다보았습니다.

"아!" 오트 대통령이 말했습니다. "뭐 . . . 사실은, 우리는 겪고 있어요 . . . 위기를 말이지요, 실은. 그래요. 그리고 익크는, 흠, 그는, 아―"

"오, 그들에게 말해요!" 오트 부인이 갑자기 울음을 터뜨렸습니다. "슈퍼-그로(Super-Gro)에 대해서요, 말해버려요, 맙소사!"

당혹스러워하며, 램참 가족은 그녀를 쳐다보았습니다. 하늘이 어두워졌고, 이제 약한 빗줄기가 내리기 시작했습니다.

"축축하네요, 네?" 앱 장군이 말했습니다. "유감스럽게도, 비를 피할 곳을 제공하지는 못하겠네요. 충분히 큰 공간이 없어요."

"스타 스카우트는 충분히 잘 맞을 거예요." 램참 부인이 말했습니다. "차를 마시러 돌아가도록 하지요."

7장 오트 대통령이 들려준 이야기

"차가 정말 도움이 되었어요. 저는 다시 진정했어요." 오트 부인이 그녀의 남편에게 고개를 끄덕였습니다. "어서요, 여보. 말해요."

비가 약하게 스타 스카우트의 위를 두드렸고, 그 안의 모습을 훨씬 더 아늑하게 보이게 했습니다. 식탁 주위로 램참 가족은 자신들의 평소 자리를 차지하고 앉았습니다. 티라인은 탁자 위에 꽂힌 압정을 스툴 삼아 앉아서, 램참 부인이 알루미늄 포일(aluminum foil)로 만들어낸 아주 작은 컵으로 마셨고, 그녀가 직접 구운 생강 쿠키(ginger snap)의 부스러기를 조금씩 먹었습니다.

이제, 한숨 쉬며, 오트 대통령이 자신의 컵을 내려놓았습니다.

"여러분은 보았을 겁니다, 램참." 그가 말했습니다. "얼마나 많이 우리가 이 맛있는 간식을 즐겼는지 말이에요. 실은, 티라에서 신선한 식품이나 마시기에 적당한 물이 완전히 사라진 지 꽤 많은 시간이 지났어요. 우리는 지금 단지 비축

해 둔 통조림이나 병에 든 것만으로 살고 있어요."

오트 부인이 얼굴을 찡그렸습니다. "분홍색 고기 스프레드, 그리고 시금치. 또 그 *끔찍한* 피졸라."

"조금 달긴 하지요, 맞아요." 앱 장군이 말했습니다. "먹으면 방귀가 나오기도 하고요. 하지만—"

"그만 말해요!" 오트 부인이 소리쳤습니다.

오트 대통령이 계속 말했습니다. "우리 비극의 원인은, 램찹, 바로 슈퍼-그로입니다. 앱 박사의 발명품이지요. 슈퍼-그로는, 앱 박사가 약속하기로는, 우리의 수확량을 두 배로 만들어주고, 그 작물 크기도 두 배로, 달콤함도 마찬가지로 두 배로 높여준다고 했지요. 훌륭한 구상이라고, 그가 말했어요."

"우리 과학자는." 앱 박사가 말했습니다. "다른 사람보다 더 크게 꿈을 꾸지요."

"3일 동안, 과학 센터에서." 오트 대통령이 계속 말했습니다. "앱은 그의 슈퍼-그로를 혼합했습니다. 온 행성에 다 퍼질 정도로, 몹시 냄새나는 통들이었죠. 하지만 그때 . . . 오, 어느 티라인도 그 네 번째 날을 결코 잊지 못할 겁니다! 저는 억스 공원을 지나 산책하고 있었어요. 얼마나 날씨가 좋던지! 나무와 풀은 정말 푸르고, 하늘은—"

"푸르다고요?" 아서가 말했습니다. "하지만 여기에 있는 모든 것이 갈색이 잖아요, 파랗지 않고요!"

"작은 사고가." 앱 박사가 중얼거렸습니다. "슈퍼-그로에 일어났어요."

"작은 사고라고?" 앱 장군이 짖듯이 말했습니다. "그 물질이 폭발했다고, 앱! 사방에 말이야!"

"뭐, 아무도 완벽하진 않으니까." 앱 박사가 부끄럽다는듯이 자신의 고개를 숙였습니다.

"그 모든 거대한 통들이 말이에요, 램찹!" 오트 대통령이 계속했습니다. "쾅! 하나씩 연달아서 터졌어요! 유리창을 산산조각 내고, 과학 센터의 지붕을 날려 버렸어요! 정말 다행스럽게도, 아무도 다치지 않았지만, 거대한 연기구름이 하늘을 까맣게 뒤덮었지요! 그러더니—그렇게 운이 나쁠 수가!—비가 오기 시작했어요. 연기와 뒤섞인, 엄청난 폭우가 티라 전 지역에 내려, 강에, 모든 들판과 정원에, 모든 녹색 식물 위로 떨어졌습니다."

자신의 압정에서 일어나서, 그는 탁자를 가로지르며 이리저리 서성거렸습니다.

"비가 그쳤을 때, 초록색이라고는 없었습니다. 아무것도요. 그냥 갈색뿐이었죠. 더 심각한 것은, 앱의 실험결과 우리의 물은 마실 수 없고, 티라의 어디에서도 그 무엇도 자랄 수 없다고 증명되었다는 겁니다. 전 즉시 국가에 방송했습니다. '절망하지 마십시오.' 제가 말했죠. '티라는 곧 일어설 것입니다.'"

"오, 세상에!" 램찹 씨가 말했습니다.

오트 대통령이 자신의 고개를 저었습니다. "전 거짓말했어요. 전 차마 진실을 말할 수가 없었어요. 알다시피, 극심한 공포를 초래하게 될까 봐 말이지요. 그 실험결과에 따르면 티라가 다시 녹색을 되찾기까지 적어도 1년이 걸린다고 합니다. 그리고 그러기 훨씬 전에 우리는 우리 마지막 통조림을, 우리의 마지막 피졸라 병을 비우게 될 것입니다."

그는 다시 앉으며, 자기 두 손으로 그의 얼굴을 가렸습니다.

"그래서 그때 우리는 . . . 우리는 메시지를 보냈습니다, 우주로요. 어떤 다른 행성의 우주선을 유혹하자, 라고 우리는 생각했어요. 그것을 인질로 잡아 몸값을 요구하는 겁니다, 있잖아요, 그들에게 식량과 물을 보내게 하는 거예요. 오, 부끄러운 일이지요! 비열하고요. 여러분은 절대 우리를 용서하지 않을 겁니다, 그래요 . . ."

그의 목소리가 점차 작아졌고, 단지 비가 후두둑 떨어지는 소리만이 들렸습니다.

금방이라도 울 것처럼, 램찹 가족은

서로를 보다가, 탁자 위에 있는 작은 사람들을 보았습니다. 티라인들은 지금 특히 더 작게, 용감하게, 그리고 훌륭하게 보였습니다.

"이 불쌍한 사람들 같으니!" 램찹 부인이 말했습니다. "우리를 정복할 필요는 없어요. 우리가 할 수 있다면, 우리가 기꺼이 여러분을 도와줄게요."

티라인들은 처음에는 자신들의 귀를 의심했습니다. 그러더니, 갑자기, 그들의 얼굴이 기쁨으로 환해졌습니다.

"감사합니다!" 앱 장군이 외쳤습니다.

"구원받았어!" 오트 부인이 손뼉 쳤습니다. "우리는 구원받았다고!"

"구원받았다니요 . . . ?" 램찹 부인이 말했습니다.

"당연하죠!" 오트 대통령이 말했습니다. "이해하지 못했나요? 지구의 우주선들이 식량과 물을 가져다줄 수 있잖아요 그때까지— 오! 왜 그래요?"

설명한 사람은 바로 아서였습니다.

"정말 미안해요." 그가 말했습니다. "하지만 단지 스타 스카우트 밖에 없어요. 지구에 다른 우주선은 없어요. 그리고 그것들을 만들려면 몇 년은 걸릴 거예요."

티라인들이 헉 하고 숨을 들이마셨습니다. "몇 년씩이나 . . . ?" 엡 박사가 말했습니다.

스탠리는 너무 슬퍼서 거의 말을 할

수가 없었습니다. "그리고 스타 스카우트를 타고 식량을 가져오는 것은 아무 소용이 없어요." 그가 말했습니다. "우리가 지구에서 돌아왔을 때쯤에는, 여러분은 모두— 흠, 알겠지만요."

"죽었겠지요." 오트 부인이 말했습니다.

스타 스카우트 안에서는, 끔찍한 침묵이 내려앉았습니다. 사실은 명확했습니다. 티라의 선반은 곧 비어버릴 것입니다. 그리고 나면 그곳의 모든 작은 사람들은 굶어 죽게 될 것입니다.

8장 스탠리의 좋은 생각

찻주전자는 이제 식었고, 마지막 쿠키 부스러기는 접시 위에 아무도 원치 않은 채 놓여 있었습니다. 스타 스카우트 내에 음울한 부위기가 마치 어두운 구름처럼 내려앉았습니다.

"이건 공평하지 않아요." 아서가 세 번이나 말했습니다. "정말 그렇지 않다고요."

"그 말 좀 그만해." 스탠리가 그에게 말했습니다. "이제 네 번이나 말했어."

"다섯 번이란다." 엡 박사가 말했습니다.

엡 장군이 기운을 내려고 했습니다. "아, 뭐 . . . 아직 통조림 고기는 좀 있

잖아요, 응? 그리고 포도 맛 피졸라도 충분하고. 고마워해야 할 일이에요."

"난 절대로 포도 맛 피졸라에 대해 고맙게 여기지 않을 거예요." 오트 부인이 말했습니다.

"그러니까 단지 . . ." 아서가 한숨 쉬었습니다. "제 말은, 지구에는 엄청 많은 식량이 있어요. 수백만 명의 사람들이 있고, 대부분 그래도 충분하잖아요."

티라인들은 깜짝 놀란 듯했습니다. "수백만 명이라고? 농담하는 거니?" 오트 대통령이 말했습니다.

"하!" 엡 장군이 말했습니다. "엄청 붐비겠네요, 내가 생각했을 땐. 수백만 명이라고요?"

램찹 부인이 미소 지었습니다. "모든 우리의 훌륭한 국가들에는, 수백만 명이 있지요. 그리고 여전히 그 수가 증가하고 있어요."

"흠, 여기도 그렇답니다." 오트 대통령이 고개를 저었습니다. "결혼한 젊은 부부들, 한 명, 두 명 출산되는 아기들이 있으니. 하지만 수백만이라니? 우리 인구는—물론, 단지 티라빌밖에 없지만—683명이지요."

"84명이에요." 오트 부인이 말했습니다. "익스 부인(Mrs. Ix)이 어젯밤에 아이를 낳았어요."

이제 놀란 사람은 바로 램찹 가족이었습니다.

"단지 티라빌밖에 없다고요?" 아서가 외쳤습니다. "하지만 티라빌은 여러분의 수도라고, 말했잖아요!"

"흠, 그럴 수밖에, 그렇지 않니, 얘야?" 오트 부인이 말했습니다.

스탠리가 자신의 고개를 저었습니다. "이 전체 행성에, 단지 684명의 티라인만 있다니! 이럴 수가, 난 장담하건대— 잠깐!"

좋은 생각이 그에게 떠올랐습니다. 스탠리는 전에도 흥분되는 생각을 한 적이 있었지만, 그 어떤 것도 이것만큼 그를 흥분되게 하지 못했습니다.

"오트 부인!" 그가 소리쳤습니다. "체중이 얼마나 나가세요?"

"스탠리!" 램찹 부인이 말했습니다.

오트 부인은 기분 나빠하지 않았습니다. "실은, 난 조금 날씬해졌단다. 비록, 슬프게도, 엉덩이는 빠지지 않았지만. 나는 6온스(6 ounces, 약 170그램)란다, 아이야. 왜 물어보니?"

스탠리에게서 말이 빠르게 나왔습니다. "왜냐하면, 만약에 부인이 평균이라면, 아이들은 심지어 더 가벼울 테고, 그럼 모든 티라인들을 합치면 무게가— 이걸 계산해 볼게요!"

"300파운드(300 pounds, 약 136킬로그램)도 나가지 않는구나." 수학을 잘하는 램찹 씨가 말했습니다. "그렇지만 나는 모르겠—" 그때 그는 깨달았습니다. "오! 훌륭하구나, 스탠리!"

"그 녀석은 똑똑하네요, 우리도 알겠어요." 앱 장군이 말했습니다. "하지만 뭔가—"

"장군님!" 램찹 씨가 말했습니다. "모든 티라인들을 여기 스타 스카우트로 불러주세요! 남아있는 통조림 음식과 포도 맛 피졸라도 가져오세요! 아마 티라가 다시 푸르게 될 때까지 지구가 여러분의 집이 될 수 있을 겁니다!"

9장 체중 측정

각각의 작은 거리에 있는 각각의 작은 집에서, 모든 남자, 여자, 그리고 아이, 심지어 교도소에서 교도관과 함께 온 익크 대위까지, 티라인들이 왔습니다. 비는 그쳤고, 작은 사람들이 모인 채 서 있는 갈색 들판 위로 저녁 불빛이 금빛으로 반짝였습니다.

오트 대통령이 그들에게 연설했습니다. "티라인 여러분! 전 여러분의 정부가 여러분을 속였다고 고백해야만 합니다! 진실은 이렇습니다: 우리의 들판과 강이 다시 회복될 때까지 적어도 1년이 걸릴 것이라고 합니다."

사람들 속에서 외침이 들렸습니다. "우리는 기만당했어요!" . . . "세상에, 이렇게 나쁜 소식이라니!" . . . "우리는 굶어 죽을 거야!" . . . "과학자들을 총살해라!"

"잠시만!" 오트 대통령이 외쳤습니다. "만약 그 여정이 가능하다면, 우리는 지구에서 피난 생활을 하라는 제안을 받았습니다! 제발, 집중해 주세요!"

앞으로 나서며, 램찹 씨가 스타 스카우트에 함께 들어 있던 작은 책자의 내용을 소리 내어 읽었습니다.

"'당신의 우주선은 편안함과 더불어 안전을 고려하여 설계되었습니다. 지시된 대로만 사용해 주세요.'" 그가 자신의 목소리를 높였습니다. "'기념품을 갖고 승선하거나 당신과 함께 타고 가자고 친구를 초대하는 행위로 무게를 더하지 마시오.'"

울음소리가 다시 나왔습니다. "저절로 끝이야!" . . . "우리는 기념품이 아니야!" . . . "그는 친구도 안 된다고 말했어, 멍청아!" . . . "우리는 끝장난 것 같네, 보아하니!"

램찹 씨가 자신의 손을 들어 올렸습니다. "아직 희망이 있어요! 하지만 여러분은 반드시 모두 체중을 측정해야만 합니다! 또 여러분이 여행에 필요한 물건들도 말이죠!"

스타 스카우트의 욕실용 체중계가, 들판에 놓였는데, 티라인들에게는 너무 높다는 것이 밝혀졌고, 아서가, 모노폴리 게임판을 사용해서, 그들이 쉽게 올

라갈 수 있도록 경사로를 만들기 전까지 잠시 체중 측정이 미뤄졌습니다.

앱 장군이 명령을 내렸습니다. "그럼, 좋아요! 20명에서 25명으로, 가족들끼리 함께 무리 지으세요! 그리고 움직이지 마세요!"

오트 가족과 다른 여섯 가족이 체중계로 올라왔는데, 그 옆에서 램찹 부인이 메모장과 연필을 들고 서 있었습니다. "7.25파운드(약 3.29킬로그램)!" 그녀가 말하면서, 받아 적었습니다.

"다음!" 앱 장군이 외쳤지만 오트 가족의 집단은 벌써 내려가고 있었고, 다른 무리가 올라오고 있었습니다.

연이어서 한 집단씩 체중계에 올랐습니다. 신이 난 아이들 때문에, 정말로 눈금이 흔들렸지만, 램찹 부인은 바늘이 멈출 때까지 주의해서 기다렸습니다. 1시간 안에 통조림 식품과 피졸라로 이루어진 물품들과 함께, 티라 전체 인구의 체중이 측정되었고, 그녀는 더했습니다.

"티라인들, 239," 그녀가 발표했습니다. "식량과 피졸라, 140. 합계: 379파운드(약 172킬로그램)예요!"

"우리는 구해질 수 있나요? 아니면 우리가 너무 뚱뚱한가요?" 한 울부짖는 소리가 말했습니다.

"말하기에는 너무 이릅니다!" 램찹 씨가 대답하며 외쳤습니다. "우리는 어떻

게 우리의 우주선을 가볍게 할 수 있을지 봐야만 해요!"

스타 스카우트의 식탁 그리고 스탠리와 아서가 수월하게 같이 침대를 쓸 수 있기에, 철제 침대 하나를 버리는 것으로 순조롭게 시작되었습니다. 그리고는 스탠리의 테니스공, 여분의 스웨터, 그리고 미국 국기가 달린 그의 주조종사 지퍼형 재킷이 그다음으로 버려졌습니다; 아서의 무릎까지 오는 양말, 우비, 그리고 그가 몰래 들고 탄 플라스틱 고릴라도 버려졌습니다. 램찹 부부는 자신들의 여분 옷, 램프, 주방용품, 모노폴리 게임, 그리고 마지막으로, 멕시코와 프랑스 포스터를 거기에 더했습니다.

그 더미의 무게가 측정되는 동안 사람들은 숨죽인 채 서 있었습니다. 어디에선가 아기가 울었고, 그의 부모가 그를 야단쳤습니다.

"377파운드(약 171킬로그램)예요!" 램찹 부인이 발표했습니다. "오, 이런!" 그녀가 오트 대통령에게 속삭였습니다. "우리가 필요한 것보다 2파운드(약 0.9킬로그램)가 더 적어요."

"알겠어요." 오트 대통령이, 잠시 생각한 후에, 체중계로 올라갔습니다. "좋은 소식입니다. 티라인 여러분!" 그가 외쳤습니다. "거의 우리 모두 구해졌습니다!"

환호성이 들리더니, 누군가 소리쳤습니다. "무슨 말이에요, *거의 모두*라니?"

"우리는, 국민 전체로서는, 조금 더 무게가 나갑니다." 오트 대통령이 설명했습니다. "하지만 만약 체격이 크다면, 단지 네 사람만, 남으면 됩니다. 내가 그 한 사람이 되겠어요. 지원자가 세 명 더 있나요?"

웅성거리는 소리가 사람들 사이에서 났습니다. "저 사람은 *내가* 원하는 바로 그런 대통령이야!" . . . "익크를 남겨 둬!" . . . "넌 어때, 랠프(Ralph)?" . . . "다른 사람한테나 물어봐, 이 미친 녀석아!"

그 문제는 빠르게 해결되었습니다. "나는 당신 없이는 가지 않을 거예요, 여보." 오트 부인이 그녀의 남편에게 말했고, 익크 대위는 인기를 다시 얻기를 바라면서, 그 자신도 역시 남겠다고 밝혔습니다.

앱 장군이 네 번째 지원자였습니다. "그냥 늙은 병사일 뿐이지요, 부인." 그가 램찹 부인에게 말했습니다. "살 만큼 살았어요, 이제 그저 사라질 때이지요, 그리고—"

"저기요! 잠깐만요!"

아서가 체중계를 가리키고 있었습니다.

"우리는 *저것*을 잊어버렸어요." 그가 말했습니다. "우리는 체중계를 두고 갈 수 있어요. 이제 아무도 남지 않아도 돼요!"

10장 집을 향해서

"익스 부부, 그리고 새로 태어난 아기는?" 오트 대통령이, 확대경 창문 위 선반에서 그의 아내 옆에 서서, 말했습니다. "아, 그래, 냉장고 위!"

티라의 사람들은 스타 스카우트의 구석구석 다양한 곳에서 할 수 있는 한 편안하게 있었습니다. 스탠리와 아서는 여행하는 동안에 티라 고등학교 학생들이 공부할 장소인 찬장을 치웠고, 램찹 부인은 침대 시트를 잘라서 수백 개의 작은 담요를 만들었고, 약간의 솜을 뜯어 베개를 만들었습니다. "임시방편이지요, 익스 부인." 그녀가 지금 말하면서, 익스 가족을 냉장고 위에 자리 잡게 했습니다. "하지만 너무나 갑작스러운 통보잖아요. 가장자리에서는 물러나세요, 알겠죠?"

"정말이지 갑작스러운 통보예요." 익스 부인이 말했습니다. "정말 많은—"

"걱정할 것 없어요." 램찹 부인이 자랑스럽게 미소 지었습니다. "내 아들인 주조종사가, 미리 연락할 거예요."

가까이 있는 선반에서, 익크 대위가 아서를 마비시키려고 했던 것에 대해 사과하며 속삭였습니다. "당신과 나(I) 사이에서 하는 이야기이지만, 난 정말로 그게 통할 거라고 생각하지 않았어요." 그가 말했습니다.

"당신과 저(me) 사이이겠지요." 램찹 부인이 말했습니다. "그렇지만 고마워요, 익크 대위." 그녀가 스탠리에게 돌아섰습니다. "우리는 모두 준비되었단다, 얘야!"

스탠리가 자신의 조종 장치를 확인했습니다. "출발합시다!"

"티라인 여러분!" 오트 대통령이 이목을 집중시키며 외쳤습니다. "우리의 국가를!"

스타 스카우트의 모든 곳에서, 티라인들이 일어섰고, 그들의 오른손을 자신의 심장 위에 얹었습니다. "흐으으으음 . . ." 오트 부인이 허밍하며, 음조를 맞췄고, 그들은 노래 부르기 시작했습니다.

"사랑스러운 행성, 티라! 자유로운 행성, 티라!

들어보렴, 사랑하는 행성아, 너에게 바치는 우리의 약속을!

우리가 어디에 가더라도, 우리가 어디에서 떠돌아다니더라도,

우리는 티라로, 우리의 고향 티라로 돌아오리라!"

그 노래가 은은하게 불이 켜진 선체 내에서 메아리쳤습니다. 많은 티라인들이 훌쩍이고 있었고, 램찹 가족의 두 눈도, 그들이 자리를 잡을 때, 역시 글썽

거렸습니다.

"아무리 보잘것없다해도, 그토록 사랑스러운 행성은 또 없다네,
우리는 언제나 티라를 사랑한다네,
멀리 떨어져 있어도 혹은—"

스탠리가 "출발" 단추를 눌렀고—부우웅!—스타 스카우트의 로켓이 작동하기 시작했습니다.

노래가 갑자기 멈췄고, 익스 부인이 냉장고에서 울부짖었습니다. "오, 맙소사! 이건 안전한가요?"

"그럼 당연하죠." 램찹 부인이 외치며 답했습니다.

"아마 그럴지도 모르죠." 익스 부인이 말했습니다. "하지만 내 생각에는 만약 티라인들이 날아야만 했다면, 우리에게 날개가 달려있었을 거예요."

부우웅! 부우웅!

스타 스카우트는 이제 떠오르며, 위로 솟으면서 속도를 얻었습니다. 그 임무는 끝났습니다. 멀리 있는 행성에서 연락했던 낯선 이들은 더 이상 낯선 사람이 아니라, 친구였습니다.

모든 것이 매우 만족스러워, 라고 스탠리는 생각했습니다. 다른 램찹 가족도 역시 그렇게 생각했습니다.

11장 다시 지구로

". . . 티라인 여러분, 당신들을 맞이하게 되어 정말로 기쁩니다." 대통령이 자신의 연설을 거의 끝맺으며, 말했습니다. "전 여러분이 지구에서 행복한 한 해를 보내길 바랍니다."

백악관 잔디 위 그의 앞에는, 사방에서 온 신문과 TV 기자들과 함께, 램찹 가족이 앉아있었고, 특별히 이 행사를 위해 만들어진 작은 특별관람석에는 티라에서 온 사람들이 있었습니다.

티라인들은 이제 정중하게 박수를 보내고 있었지만, 그들은 긴장한 듯 보였고, 램찹 부인은 그 이유를 짐작할 수 있었습니다. 스타 스카우트의 착륙을 위해 우주 센터에 모여든 사람들하며, 워싱턴 D.C.까지 이어지는 사람들로 붐비는 길을 지나온 것까지! 가여운 티라인들! 그들이 보든 모든 곳에, 거대한 건물, 거대한 사람들이 있었습니다. 그들이 어떻게 이곳에서 편안함을 느낄 수 있겠어요?

하지만 깜짝 놀랄 일이 기다리고 있었습니다. 잔디 저편에, 큰 하얀 천이 펼쳐져 있었습니다. 이제, 대통령의 신호에 따라, 인부들이 천을 당겨 걷어냈습니다.

"환영합니다." 대통령이 말했습니다. "티라빌 2입니다!"

헉 하고 숨을 들이마시는 소리가 티라인들 사이에서 나더니, 환희에 찬 외침이 나왔습니다.

그들 앞에는, 백악관 테니스 코트였던 것 위에, 각각의 티라인 가족당 하나씩 주어진, 작은 집들이, 가게와 학교들 그리고 교회들, 또 모든 주요 거리를 지나가는 미니어처 철도와 함께 놓여 있었습니다. 스탠리가 우주에서 미리 연락했을 때부터 시작되었던 것으로, 워싱턴과 뉴욕에 있는 주요 장난감 상점들에서 보내온 긴급 배송 덕분에, 티라빌 2는 스타 스카우트가 도착하기 훨씬 전에 완성되었습니다.

흥분한 티라인들이 특별관람석에서 달려가서 자신들의 새 집을 살펴보았고, 곧 티라빌 2에 있는 모든 창문과 문가에서 행복해하는 목소리가 나왔습니다. "멋진 가구야!" . . . "만세! 신선한 레모네이드야! 더는 피졸라는 먹지 않아도 돼!" . . . "벽장 안에, 봤어? 셔츠, 드레스, 정장, 신발이 있어!" . . . "심지어, 속옷도 있어!"

오트 부부, 앱 장군, 엡 박사, 그리고 익크 대위는 작별 인사를 하러 다시 왔고, 램찹 가족은 무릎을 꿇고 손가락 끝을 건드리며 인사했습니다. TV 연출진들이 이를 촬영했고, 아서는 익크 대위가 만지자 마비된 것처럼 흉내 내어 모든 사람을 웃게 했습니다. 그리고는 기

자들이 떠났고, 티라인들도 티라빌 2로 돌아갔고, 단지 대통령만이 램찹 가족과 함께 백악관 잔디 위에 남았습니다.

"흠, 다시 일하러 가야겠네요." 대통령이 한숨 쉬었습니다. "잘 가요, 램찹 가족. 알다시피, 여러분은 모두 영웅입니다. 한 나라를 구했어요."

"그렇지는 않아요." 스탠리가 말했습니다. "그들이 우리를 정복할 수 없었을 뿐이에요."

"뭐, 여러분은 제가 무슨 말을 하는지 알잖아요." 대통령이 말했습니다. "여러분 남아서 저녁 식사를 같이할래요?"

"고맙지만, 사양하겠어요." 램찹 부인이 말했습니다. "꽤 늦었고, 오늘은 흥미로웠지만 몹시 피곤한 하루였거든요."

그들이 집에 도착했을 땐 잠자리에 들 시간이었습니다. 스탠리와 아서는 그들이 잠을 자는 데 도움이 될 따뜻한 코코아와 함께, 가볍게 저녁 식사를 했고, 그 이후에 램찹 부부가 그들에게 이불을 잘 덮어주고 잘 자라고 인사했습니다.

형제는 잠시 어둠 속에서 조용히 누워 있었습니다. 그때 아서가 낄낄 웃었습니다.

"마그노-타이타닉 마취총은 정말 무섭기는 했어." 그가 말했습니다. "용감했어, 스탠리 형, 나를 보호해주다니."

"마음 쓰지 마." 스탠리가 말했습니

다. "넌 내 동생이잖아, 그렇지?"

"나도 알지만 . . ." 아서는 이제 졸렸습니다. "스탠리 형? 티라인들이 돌아갈 때, 그들의 땅과 물은 괜찮아질까? 그들이 우리에게 알려줄까?"

"그럴 것 같아." 스탠리도 또한, 졸렸습니다. "잘 자, 아서."

"잘 자." 아서가 말했고, 곧 그들은 둘 다 잠이 들었습니다.

그리고 시간이 흘러, 저 멀고 먼 광활한 우주 저편에서, 하지만 더는 낯설지도 미지의 장소도 아닌 먼 곳에서, 또 다른 메시지가 왔습니다.

"우리는 고향에 왔습니다. 모든 것이 괜찮아요."

그리고 또다시 왔지요.

"우리는 집에 왔어요! 고마워요, 지구! 모든 것이 다 괜찮아요!"

끝

Chapter 1

1. C "Isn't this nice, George?" said Mrs. Lambchop, stirring paste. "No excitement. A perfectly *usual* day." Mr. Lambchop knew just what she meant. Excitement was often troublesome.

2. B "Lambchop residence?" said the caller. "The President of the United States speaking. Who's this?" Stanley smiled. "The King of France." "They don't have kings in France. Not anymore." "Excuse me, but I'm too busy for jokes." Stanley kept his eyes on the TV. "My brother and I are watching the *Tom Toad Show*."

3. A The screen showed the President, looking very serious, behind his desk. "My fellow Americans," the President said. "I am sorry to interrupt this program, but someone out there doesn't realize that I am a very busy man who can't waste time joking on the telephone. I hope the particular person I am talking to—and I do not mean the King of France!—will remember that. Thank you."

4. C "Stanley!" exclaimed Mrs. Lambchop. "The King of France indeed!" "Gosh!" Arthur said. "Will Stanley get put in jail?" "There is no law against being a telephone smarty," Mr. Lambchop said. "Perhaps there should be."

5. D "I had to be sure," said the President. "We have to get together, Lambchop! I'll send my private plane right now, fetch you all here to Washington, D.C." Mr. Lambchop gasped. "Private plane? Washington? *All* of us?" "The whole family." The President chuckled.

Chapter 2

1. D "Tyrra! Never heard of it, right?" The Lambchops all shook their heads. "*Nobody* ever heard of it. It's a planet, up there somewhere. They sent a message, the first ever from outer space!" The Lambchops were greatly interested. "Imagine!" Mrs. Lambchop exclaimed. "What did it say?" "Very friendly tone," the President said. "Peaceful, just checking around. Asked us to visit."

2. C "Ah, yes! The *Star Scout*!" He leaned forward. "That's our new top-secret spaceship, just ready now!"

3. A Mr. Lambchop drew in a deep breath. "Mr. President, why *Stanley*?" "It has to be someone who's already had adventure experience," the President said. "Well, my Secret Service showed me a newspaper story about when Stanley was flat and caught two robbers. Robbers! That's adventure!"

4. B "We sent the *Star Scout* up again, this time with our cleverest trained bird aboard. But hear for yourself." The President spoke into a little box on his desk. "Send in Dr. Schwartz, please." A bearded man entered, wearing a white coat and carrying a birdcage with a cloth over it. Bowing, he removed the cloth to reveal a large, brightly colored parrot. "Thank you, Herman," the President said. "Dr. Schwartz is our top space scientist," he told the Lambchops, "and this is Polly, the bird I spoke of."

5. D "Would it be possible, Mr. President, for us all to go?" "Well, if you don't mind the crowding," the President said. "And skimping on baggage." "Actually, we had in mind the seaside," Mr. Lambchop said. "Or a tennis camp. But—" The Queen of England looked in again. "May we ask if—" "Just a *minute*, for heaven's sake!" said the President. "We shall return anon." Looking peeved, the Queen went away. Mr. Lambchop had decided. "Mr. President, the seaside will keep. We will go to Tyrra, sir."

Chapter 3

1. B The countdown had begun. When it reached "zero," Chief Pilot Stanley Lambchop would press the "Start" button, and the Star Scout would blast off for Tyrra.

2. B Stanley was wondering if the Tyrrans would mind that Earth had sent just an ordinary family. Suppose they were big stuck-ups and expected a general or a TV star, or even the President?

3. C Mr. Lambchop was thinking that serving one's country was noble, but this was a bit much. How did these things happen? Off to an unknown planet, the entire family!

4. D Mrs. Lambchop thought that Mr. Lambchop seemed fretful. But why, now that the *Star Scout* looked so *nice?* Thanks to her, in fact. "They may call it a spaceship," she had said when she first saw it, "but where's the space? Just one room! And all gray . . . ? Drab, I say!" Much of the training at the Space Center, however, was physical, and Mrs. Lambchop, who jogged and exercised regularly, quickly passed the tests required. In the days that followed, while the others were being made fit, she used her free time to make the *Star Scout* more like home.

5. A Arthur, by nature lazy, was thinking that he was glad to be done with all the jogging, jumping, climbing ladders, and scaling walls.

Chapter 4

1. A The third evening they appeared on TV news broadcasts on Earth. Word of their voyage had been released to the press, and all over the world people were eager to learn how this extraordinary adventure was proceeding. Standing before the spaceship's camera, the Lambchops said they felt fine, looked forward to meeting the Tyrrans, and would report nightly while they remained in TV range.

2. B "Happy birthday, Stanley Lambchop! I've arranged a surprise. First, your friends from school." There was silence for a moment, broken only by the clearing of throats, and then, from all the millions of miles away, came the voices of Stanley's classmates singing, "Happy Birthday, dear Stanley! Happy Birthday to you!"

3. D The screen had gone blank. They had traveled too far. There would be no more voices from Earth, no voices but their own until they heard what the Tyrrans had to say.

4. C "Right," said the Tyrran voice. "Keep going till you pass a star formation that looks like a foot. You can't miss it. Then, just past a lopsided little white moon, start down. You'll see a pointy mountain, then a big field. Land there."

5. B Suddenly a message came, but not the sort they expected. "Surrender,

Earth people!" said the radio. "Your spaceship is trapped by our unbreakable trapping cable! You are prisoners of Tyrra! Surrender!"

Chapter 5

1. D A thin blue line, like a thread, had been passed over the *Star Scout*. Stanley switched on the wiper above the big window and the first flick of its blade parted the blue line.

2. C The Tyrran messenger came slowly forward to stand before the big window, a muscular, scowling young man with a curling mustache, wearing shorts and carrying a club. The mustache was very large. The messenger was not. "That man," Mrs. Lambchop said slowly, "is only three inches tall." "At most," Mr. Lambchop said.

3. C "... afraid to let us see you, Earth people? Because I'm so enormous? Hah! *All* Tyrrans are this big!"

4. B "I am General Ap!" shouted the uniformed man. "Commander of all Tyrran forces!" Stanley stepped forward. "Chief Pilot Stanley Lambchop," he said. "From Earth. These are my parents, Mr. and Mrs. George Lambchop. And my brother, Arthur." "President Ot of Tyrra, and Mrs. Ot," said General Ap, indicating the wavy-haired man and the lady. "The bald chap is Dr. Ep, our scientist. The grouchy one with the flag is my aide, Captain Ik."

5. A President Ot raised his hand. "No harm done! Come! TyrraVille, our capital, is but a stroll away." The Lambchops, equipped now with handy magnifying lenses from the *Star Scout*'s science kit, followed the committee.

Chapter 6

1. B Except for its size, and the lack of greenness, the Tyrran capital was indeed much like a small village on Earth. A Main Street bustled with Tyrrans shopping and running errands; there were handsome school and public buildings, two churches with spires as high as Mr. Lambchop's waist, and side streets of pretty houses with lawns like neat brown postage stamps.

2. D The tour caused a great stir. Everywhere the tiny citizens of TyrraVille waved from windows and rooftops. At the Science Center, the last stop, journalists took photographs, and the Lambchops were treated to Grape Fizzola, the Tyrran national drink, hundreds of bottles of which were emptied into four tubs to make Earth-size portions.

3. A "Surrender!" he shouted. "You cannot resist our Magno-Titanic Paralyzer Ray! Tyrra will yet be saved!"

4. C Yellow light flickered up at Arthur from the Magno-Titanic Paralyzer. "Yikes!" said Arthur, as shrieks rose from the crowd. But it was not on Arthur that the Magno-Titanic beam landed. Stanley had sprung forward to protect his brother, and the light shone now on his chest and shoulders.

5. D Stanley was smiling. The yellow rays still flickering upon him, he rolled his head and wiggled his hands to show that he was fine. "It's nice, actually," he said. "Like a massage." The crowd hooted. "It only works on people Tyrran-size!" someone called.

Chapter 7

1. C "The fact is, Tyrra has for some time been totally without fresh food or water fit to drink. We live now only by what tins and bottles we had in store."

2. A President Ot continued. "The cause of our tragedy, Lambchops, was Super-Gro. An invention of Dr. Ep's. Super-Gro, Ep promised, would double our crops, make them double size, double delicious as well. A great concept, he said."

3. C "And then—such dreadful luck!—it began to rain. A *tremendous* rain, mixing with the smoke, falling all over Tyrra, into the rivers, on to every field and garden, every bit of greenery." Rising from his thumbtack, he paced back and forth across the table. "When the rain stopped, there was no green. None. Just brown. Worse, Ep's tests proved that our water was undrinkable, and that nowhere on Tyrra would anything grow."

4. A "So then we . . . We sent a message, into space. Lure some other planet's

spaceship, we thought. Hold it for ransom, you see, make them send food and water. Oh, shameful! Underhanded. You will never forgive us, I know . . ."

5. D "Of course!" said President Ot. "Don't you see? Earth's spaceships can bring food and water till—Oh! What's wrong?" It was Arthur who explained. "I'm very sorry," he said. "But there's just the Star Scout. Earth hasn't got any other spaceships. And it would take years to build them."

Chapter 8

1. B Gloom hung like a dark cloud within the *Star Scout.*

2. C "It's just that . . ." Arthur sighed. "I mean, Earth has so *much* food. Millions of people, and there's mostly still enough." The Tyrrans seemed amazed. "Millions? You're joking?" said President Ot. "Hah!" said General Ap. "Dreadful crush, I should think. Millions?"

3. A "Our population—there's just TyrraVille, of course—is six hundred and eighty-three." "Eighty-four," said Mrs. Ot. "Mrs. Ix had a baby last night." Now it was the Lambchops who were amazed. "Just TyrraVille?" Arthur cried. "But TyrraVille's your *capital*, you said!" "Well, it would have to be, wouldn't it, dear?" said Mrs. Ot. Stanley shook his head. "On the whole planet, only six hundred and eighty-four Tyrrans!"

4. B "Mrs. Ot!" he shouted. "How much do you weigh?" "Stanley!" said Mrs. Lambchop. Mrs. Ot was not offended. "Actually, I've slimmed a bit. Though not, sadly, in the hips. I'm six ounces, young man. Why do you ask?" The words rushed out of Stanley. "Because if you're average, only children would be even lighter, then all the Tyrrans put together would weigh—Let me figure this out!"

5. C "General!" said Mr. Lambchop. "Summon all Tyrrans here to the *Star Scout!* Fetch what remains of your tinned food and Grape Fizzola! Perhaps Earth can be your home till Tyrra is green again!"

Chapter 9

1. A Stepping forward, Mr. Lambchop read aloud from the booklet that had come with the *Star Scout*. "'Your spacecraft has been designed for safety as well as comfort. Use only as directed.'" He raised his voice. "'Do not add weight by bringing souvenirs aboard *or by inviting friends to ride with you*.'"

2. D General Ap barked orders. "Right, then! Groups of twenty to twenty-five, families together! And don't jiggle!"

3. C "Tyrrans, two hundred and thirty-nine," she announced. "Food and Fizzola, one hundred and forty. Total: Three hundred and seventy-nine pounds!" "Are we saved? Or are we too fat?" came a cry. "Too soon to tell!" Mr. Lambchop called back. "We must see how we can lighten our ship!" A good start was made by discarding the *Star Scout*'s dining table and one steel bunk, since Stanley and Arthur could easily share.

4. B A good start was made by discarding the *Star Scout*'s dining table and one steel bunk, since Stanley and Arthur could easily share. Then out went Stanley's tennis balls, extra sweater, and his Chief Pilot zip jacket with the American flag; out went Arthur's knee socks, raincoat, and a plastic gorilla he had smuggled aboard. Mr. and Mrs. Lambchop added their extra clothing, lamps, kitchenware, the Monopoly game, and at last, the posters of Mexico and France.

5. D "We weigh, as a nation, a bit too much," President Ot explained. "But only four, if largish, need stay behind. I shall be one. Will three more volunteer?"

Chapter 10

1. C The people of Tyrra were being made as comfortable as possible in the various nooks and crannies of the *Star Scout*.

2. B Stanley and Arthur had cleared a cupboard where Tyrra High School students could study during the trip, and Mrs. Lambchop had cut up sheets to make hundreds of little blankets, and put out bits of cotton for pillows.

3. D From a nearby shelf, Captain Ik whispered an apology for attempting to paralyze Arthur.

4. C The words echoed in the softly lit cabin. Many Tyrrans were weeping, and the eyes of the Lambchops, as they took their seats, glistened too.

5. A The *Star Scout* lifted now, gaining speed as it rose. Its mission was done. The strangers who had called from a distant planet were no longer strangers, but friends. It was all very satisfactory, Stanley thought.

Chapter 11

1. A The Tyrrans were now applauding politely, but they looked nervous, and Mrs. Lambchop guessed why. That crowd at the Space Center for the *Star Scout*'s landing, that drive through crowded streets into Washington, D.C.! Poor Tyrrans! Everywhere they looked, giant buildings, giant people. How could they feel comfortable here?

2. B Before them, on what had been the White House tennis court, lay an entire village of tiny houses, one for each Tyrran family, with shops and schools and churches, and a miniature railway serving all principal streets.

3. D Begun when Stanley called ahead from space, TyrraVille Two had been completed well before the *Star Scout*'s arrival, thanks to rush deliveries from leading toy stores in Washington and New York.

4. C "Well, you know what I mean," the President said. "You folks care to stay for supper?" "Thank you, no," Mrs. Lambchop said. "It is quite late, and this has been an exciting but very tiring day." It was bedtime when they got home.

5. D And in time, from the great farness of space, but a farness no longer strange or unknown, another message came. *"We are home. All is well."*